Britain in Play:
Stories and Skits for ESL

Barry Nicholson

Starhands Publishing

Paradise

CONTENTS

LIST OF PLAY SCRIPTS

Introduction

Welcome to Britain

Britain is a fascinating and diverse country, perfectly located in western Europe. In this book you will find sixteen stories from Britain's rich cultural history. Importantly, each story is accompanied by a play script designed for young learners. Children and teens will enjoy acting out the skits, and will wake up to the joys of British stories through practical drama and literature.

Stories and tales were originally oral, then written forms were passed down from generation to generation, from grandfather to grandson, from grandmother to granddaughter. As technology developed with the use of printed, audio and electronic media, the tales have come to be more widely distributed and appreciated.

With this in mind, it is the aim of this book to enlighten the reader and their students of Britain's rich heritage by presenting a variety of stories and skits grouped according to theme. These stories remind us of the many traditions at work within the British nation in relation to its kings, celebrities, inventors and animals.

Play, Story and Skit

A few words in the book's title need defining: play, story and skit. The definitions have been drawn from various online dictionaries (see the reference list at the back of the book for details).

Play: In a theatrical sense, it is a piece of writing intended to be acted in a theatre or similar place of performance; it is a dramatic work for stage or to be broadcast. An intriguing alternative definition sees 'play' as a light or brisk, constantly changing movement, as in 'a play of light'; or on an even higher level as freedom of action or activity, as in 'a full play of the mind'. Whereas I do not expect our students to encounter this higher state of being, it would, however, be nice if their creative juices were squeezed and stretched a little.

Story: We often ask our students to write a story or order a sequence of events so that they make sense, and we usually use the past simple to achieve this. Essentially, a 'story' is a narrative, either true of fictional, designed to interest, amuse, or instruct the reader; and this is often a connected series of events that can be either true or imagined.

Skit: A 'skit' is a satirical or humorous story or sketch, especially one done by amateurs. It derives from the word 'sketch', and is often a comedic segment of a show or performance that often makes a joke of something. Certainly this element of humour is a theme that crops up throughout this book, and your children or teens will no doubt be eager to tap in to this valuable way of viewing the world at large.

A lot of the definitions suggest some kind of public performance, for example on TV or radio. Though I realise this is beyond the capability of most of us in the classroom or community centre, it may be possible to experiment with a video camera or other audio-visual recording device as resources and technology allow. Failing that, a well-rehearsed public performance will certainly do!

Scope and style

This book is primarily aimed at parents, teachers, and youth community leaders and their child or children, but there is also much of interest to the general reader. The stories and skits are written in a simple and enjoyable way, but do not patronise the reader or student.

Thankfully English is an art, not a science; it is descriptive rather than prescriptive; it is a creative and cultural act. Throughout, the English language is taken as a creative being; an abstract entity that can be neither seen nor heard except in its manifestation as the written word or spoken utterance. This is expressed no more so than in a short play or skit. And, as Shakespeare would have it, "all the world's a stage, and all the men and women mere players" ('As You Like It' Act II Scene VII).

I want to motivate and inspire – that means teachers, parents and youth leaders as well as children and teens – and it is in this light that this book has been written. Though it does not claim to be *the* answer, or even *an* answer, the book does claim to be a *way*, a way to approach your lessons or study period through literature, stories and drama.

The real question is one of motivation, of getting students motivated to study, and to help them help their peers to success too. The skills our youngsters get in these early days will help propel them into the future – their future – towards high school, university and beyond. As they progress through time, the study skills, methods and motivation techniques we show them now will stick with them and be added to and developed by them; education, drama and story-telling skills that will stay with and guide them, that they themselves can pass on to others.

Students can then progress in their studies with a sense of purpose and confidence.

Structure and Layout

Each unit follows the same basic pattern. After the title there is a short summary of the story called 'In Brief'. Here, the story is told, mostly in past simple and in prose. It is designed to be read either in one's head or out loud, perhaps before an audience or class of students in assembly.

Then the play script itself. First there is a list of characters that appear in the play – some are human, some animals, and some things. Then the setting is given, which gives ideas for scenery; then the script. I have tried to keep stage directions to a minimum or, in some circumstances not at all, when directions are obvious and so obsolete.

As a parent, teacher or youth leader, it is your creative juices that are equally as important as the children's, and so you should feel free to adapt or add to the presented materials if you judge it to be correct, according to your opinion, resources, and working environment.

The Stories

The stories are divided into four main themes:

- ❖ Animals and Beasts
- ❖ Music and Popular Culture
- ❖ Kings, Queens and Royalty
- ❖ Moments and Events

Each theme presents four stories (and following them, four plays or skits). In more detail the sixteen units are:

1. Famous Animals

    Who doesn't like animals? Famous animals come from all around the world, and here I focus on some of the very best from Britain;

2. Dick Whittington and his Cat

    One of the most famous characters in British folklore, he overcame poverty and 'turned again' to become Lord Mayor of London – alongside his cat;

3. A Tale of Two Dragons

    Taking their place in mythology are two important British dragons: the poisonous dragon that St. George killed, and the proud Welsh dragon;

4. Looking for Nessie

    If we are to believe the various photos, films, sonar records and sightings then there really is a dinosaur-style monster in the depths of Loch Ness;

5. The Beatles

By far the biggest phenomenon in the western world during the 1960s was The Beatles, a hugely popular music group from Liverpool, England;

6. Winning the Eurovision Song Contest

The contest has the aim of fostering greater partnership between European nations, but with a mix of unusual costumes and painfully smiling faces it lends itself to ridicule;

7. A Visit to Madame Tussauds

Have you ever met Her Majesty Queen Elizabeth II, Donald Trump, or a sports star like Ronaldo? Your chance is here at this life-like wax museum;

8. Sherlock Holmes

Perhaps the most famous detective of all time is Sir Arthur Conan Doyle's Sherlock Holmes, with his line: "It's elementary, my dear Watson".

9. Henry VIII and his Six Wives

King Henry VIII is known for his succession of wives, some of whom met a deadly fate and return from time to time as ghosts;

10. King Harold and the Battle of Hastings

1066 was an important year in British history: William the Conqueror invaded, and King Harold died at the Battle of Hastings after he was shot in the eye with an arrow;

11. Mary, Queen of Scots
   *Though she had a kind and likeable temperament, Queen Mary
   had little political or managerial ability – a flaw that led to her
   downfall;*

12. The Murder of Thomas Becket
   *The murder of Thomas Becket remains one of the most important
   events of medieval Britain, and shows how two friends can
   become enemies with catastrophic results;*

13. The Great Fire of London
   *Here we focus on the Great Fire of 1666 which started in the King's
   bakers in Pudding Lane, near the City of London;*

14. Famous Inventions
   *Britain is a very inventive place, and some of the world's greatest
   inventions are British. Here, five of them are showcased;*

15. Crazy Sports and Contests
   *To say Britain is a nation of eccentrics is an understatement: just
   take a glance at these obsessive and bird-brained sports and
   contests;*

16. The Titanic
   *RMS Titanic was famed for its luxurious fittings and wealthy
   passengers. However, on its maiden voyage it hit an iceberg and
   sank with the loss of many lives.*

The Props / Costume Box

Children and teens have great imagination and, at this level, simple props and costumes will do. Let us look at the two concepts – props and costumes – in turn, and note how, for our purposes, the 'props box' and 'costume box' are one and the same.

Props are an essential part of any staged performance, and can be elaborate and complicated or as simple as a table and chair. Usually a skit or short play designed for (or written by) children or teens will veer towards the latter, making use of whatever is in the classroom or community centre. That is not to say that a few well-chosen and placed props would not enhance the performance. Think plastic daggers and tomato ketchup for a murder-mystery, for example.

Sharman (2004: 59) identifies a 'props table'. She defines a 'prop' as "practically everything on the set that is not nailed down – from the pictures on the walls to the contents of a handbag". Sharman divides props into the following categories:

1. Furniture – tables, chairs, sofas, beds, etc.;
2. Glass (and Pottery) – bottles, glasses, flower pots, etc.;
3. Food & Drink – both real and fake;
4. Flowers & Plants – as part of the set, or as part of the play;
5. Personal Props – eg. the contents of a handbag, or cigarettes.

To which I add:

1. Classroom-related Props – desks, chairs, blackboard, etc.;

2. Breakable or Broken Props – that may be broken as part of the script (eg. a jug thrown to the floor);
3. Intellectual Props – things spoken about but not seen;
4. People as Props – eg. children dressed as trees in the background;
5. Wearable Props – eg. a pair of glasses, or a wig.

Let's move on to the 'costume' part of the box. As I mentioned before (and as you will no doubt already know), children and teens have a marvellous capacity for creativity and imagination. At this level simple costumes, often just one or two fancy dressing-up clothes, if anything, will do. The question of make-up will probably not arise at all.

So, keep it simple – the simpler the better – and remember that you only have to *suggest* a character by their appearance: you're not going for a Hollywood Oscar.

Take the example of 'The Beatles'. You only need to *suggest* to the audience that the four spotty teens standing in front of you are The Beatles – the audience's imagination will do the rest! You may need, for example:

❖ fake or toy guitars – you can find a guitar shape on the net or from a book and copy it onto and cut it out of cardboard;
❖ a fake or toy drum – if your budget is limited, think baked bean can or bucket;
❖ 'Beatle' wigs – again, if budget is limited, think crepe paper cut into strips and fastened at the top, or mop heads;
❖ fake cigarettes – use pencils or sticks;
❖ colourful tie – from the local charity shop, or borrow one from your father;
❖ fake moustaches – made from thick black paper;

❖ thick outdoor coats (for the closing scene on Apple Corps roof) – just use your own regular coats;
❖ long-hair 'Beatle' wigs – again, think crepe paper.

For our purposes the prop box and costume box are combined. I'd recommend you get an old (large) cardboard box from the local supermarket, or arrange all the bits and bobs on a table (as Sharman suggests). I prefer a large cardboard box because it is portable and introduces an element of 'lucky dip'.

If you really want to make a professional go of it, you can assign a 'props table', labelled as such, marking it out with masking tape according to scene. In our example 'The Beatles', most of the props and costumes are the same throughout the scenes, so it is not necessary to lay them out scene-by-scene, but instead 'all in one go'. You could go so far as to label each area of the table according to what prop or costume piece should be placed there. Laying out the table can be assigned as the job for the 'props team'.

Lighting and Sound Effects

Lighting, in a short children or teen's play performed in front of peers, may not be a consideration at all. But a few of the skits presented in this book could do with a sprinkle of lighting effects so to enhance dramatic effect. I am primarily thinking of a couple of examples.

The first is 'The Great Fire of London'. Obviously, some suggestion of fire is necessary. You could wave large bits of red and orange sugar paper in the air to great effect, but if you are able, some kind of lighting technique is far preferable. Hmmm, lighting on a limited budget? Well, it's possible! The simplest way is to put a piece of coloured plastic in front of a torch or flashlight, with the main lights in the room turned down or the curtains drawn. The torches can be waved around for suitable effect. Maybe you are lucky enough to have a school or community centre stage that has a set of lights. Well, in this case the sky is the limit, but don't forget to practice a lot before the performance!

My second example comes from the play 'The Murder of Thomas Becket'. At the end of the last scene, the King repents the sad loss of his once-good friend Thomas Becket, and falls to his knees in sorrow. Stage directions call for the lights to fade. Well, again, if you have the facility then by all means fade out the lights. The rest of us can make do with the main light being switched off, or the curtains drawn at the suitable moment by able assistants. At the very least the floor assistants could draw the stage curtains or hold up a sheet or blanket!

I am not anticipating that your students will use sound effects other than the very simplest. You might, for example, use a hand-bell to signify the ring of the church bells in 'Dick Whittington and his Cat', or the taped roar of a monster in 'Looking for Nessie'. Some of the plays involve several scenes, and the gaps between them (when costumes and furniture are being changed) could be filled with interlude music such as between the scenes in 'The Beatles'. But sound effects and music for our purposes are a luxury, not a necessity.

The Director's Corner

The 'Director' could either be you, as the student's mentor, teacher, or community group leader, or it could be one of the students themselves.

If students are to work in small groups and write and produce their own play or skit then the role of the director is far less important. On the other hand, if there is to be a final performance in front of parents and/or peers, then the choice of a confident director who can, literally, direct, becomes paramount. I think that within the scope of this book, it can be assumed that the 'adult' will be named the director.

OK, so what kind of things does a director do? Essentially, they plan the whole thing from start to finish, from choice of who plays what part, to saying who stands or moves where on stage. This is not to say that the children or teens will have no say in anything – on the contrary, it is partially the director's role to listen to and incorporate ideas and suggestions if they are appropriate. But at the end of the day, the director has the final say.

Take a look at some of the sub-sections of the introduction: the props and costume box, the lighting and sound effects, the set design, and also matters such as getting everyone in the right place at the right time, someone falling ill and not being able to take part, or a change of classroom or venue at the last moment. These are all the responsibility of the director. So, the director must have a firm overview of proceedings and a clear idea of 'the big picture'.

It depends on your circumstances, of course, but sometimes the students can be set up in small groups of, say, four or five, and told to get on with it by themselves. It is a good idea in this case to give the students some guidance as to how to go about the task, maybe a printed handout with a sequence of things to do: name of the play, character list, who is to be set and scenery manager, costume designer, script writer, and so on. It is a good idea for the group to elect a 'group leader' from the outset – a kind of pseudo-director.

Whoever is directing, or leading, someone will have to come up with some sort of a basic set. I'm not suggesting lavish backdrops lit with super-troopers and glitterballs (can you imagine?) – a table and chair will do. You might like to mock up some hills behind Dick Whittington, or some front doors behind Sherlock Holmes, for example. Keep it simple, and remember that what the audience can see from the pits is less defined compared to what you can all see on stage!

Moving Forward

As I sit and write this book I am in London. Great Britain is a lovely place, chaotic and charming at the same time. I would recommend anyone to visit, especially with children. They will love coming face to face with the stars at Madame Tussauds, climbing the Monument in Pudding Lane, searching for Nessie, or visiting the Belfast Titanic museum. Most of the stories in this book have a geographical location, and as such most places can be visited with the effect that the stories and plays come to life!

What more can I say? Enjoy this collection of diamonds from Britain's past, and all things considered your children and teens will enjoy them too.

Barry Nicholson
London 2017

PURE
WILD!

Famous Animals

In Brief

Who doesn't like animals? Kids, teens and adults alike find fascination and comfort in our little (and big) friends, and it has been proven that human contact with animals reduces stress and anxiety, and lowers blood pressure and heart rate. Famous animals come from all round the world, but here I focus on some of the very best from Britain.

Many of the most famous have lived in London Zoo, located within Regent's Park in London. Top of the list are two very special animals, both very different. Guy the gorilla was born on Guy Fawkes Day 1947 (hence the name) and arrived at the zoo as a baby, clutching a mini hot water bottle. You can easily find this image on the internet as it is very famous. He became instantly popular with an adoring public, who travelled from afar to see him. When sparrows entered his enclosure, he would scoop them up gently, peer at them, then let them go. Cute! After he died in 1978, a statue was erected near his old enclosure that visitors can see to this day.

In 1965 another of London Zoo's animals shot to fame – Goldie, the golden eagle. Why? Because the plucky bird managed to escape and spent a total of eleven days, 19½ hours 'on the run' in Regent's Park before finally being coaxed back to the zoo by friendly zookeepers. Such was Goldie's fame that he was cheered every time he was mentioned in the House of Commons, and 5,000 spectators caused traffic jams and havoc around Regent's Park as they flocked to try and see him. More animals from London Zoo later.

Eros was a wild snowy owl who got lost at sea near the Azores, mid-Atlantic. He fell exhausted onto the deck of HMS Eros (hence the name) where the crew took him as their mascot. He lived for many years and fathered 57 chicks with three different mates before his sad death in 1993.

Belinda was a Mexican red-kneed bird-eating spider who, despite appearances, was very human-friendly and became very popular with the public. She made countless TV appearances, helping people overcome their fear of spiders, and as part of hypnotherapy programmes. She also died in 1993, aged 22 years.

Back to London Zoo, Winnie was an American black bear donated to the zoo at the outbreak of World War I in 1914. She was often visited by the author A.A. Milne and his son Christopher, and was the inspiration for Winnie the Pooh and Christopher Robin.

Staying on a bear theme, Brumas was a polar bear born on 27th November 1949, named after her keepers Bruce and Sam. She was apparently the first polar bear to be successfully raised in Britain, and caused much interest – London Zoo's attendance skyrocketed by one million in the year 1950, for example. She was the inspiration for many souvenirs, books, and toys – we have her to thank for the gift shops we always see at visitor attractions around the world. Pipaluk ("the little one") was another polar bear at the zoo, born on 1st December 1967. He attracted many spectators until he left in 1985 to retire to a zoo in Poland.

Jumbo the elephant was born in 1861 and, along with his companion Alice, were trained to give people of all ages rides on their backs. This was quite amazing as the elephants were each 11 feet tall. What a view! Jumbo and his companion were well-known for their playful nature, stealing people's hats before gently replacing them on their owner's heads. Sadly, he died in 1885, but his name lives on in the form of those giant flying machines, 'jumbo jets'.

Back at sea, Unsinkable Sam was a cat who was just that – unsinkable. During World War II he survived three great ship sinkings. First, the German ship Bismarck which sank on 27th May 1941; then he was saved by the HMS Cossack which itself sank on 24th October that same year; and Sam's last ship, HMS Ark Royal was again sunk off Gibraltar. Apparently she was rescued "angry but quite unharmed". Unsinkable indeed.

Well, that was an unsinkable cat. But how about an unsinkable pig? That's just who Tirpitz was. She was saved from the German ship SMS Dresden when it sank in 1915, by the HMS Glasgow. One of the crew risked his life to jump in to rescue her, and the over-sized pig became the ship's mascot. Though she died soon after the end of the war, she was stuffed and donated to the Imperial War Museum.

Gustav was a carrier pigeon in World War II, used by the RAF to send messages back home across enemy lines. On 6th June 1944, for example, he carried news back of the first D-Day landings in Normandy. He flew more than 150 miles (241km) from northern France to Portsmouth, England. His flight took just over five hours. What important D-Day message did he bring? That the allied vessels were just 20 miles off the Normandy coast, with no visible signs of German interference or counter-attack. For his work during the war he was awarded the Dickin Medal – and so takes the number of pigeons that have been awarded the medal to 32, more than any other species, apparently.

Two great horses complete the list of animals. Warrior was a World War I horse ridden by Captain Jack Seely, serving throughout the entire war. For example, leading the Canadian Cavalry Brigade, they fought at Moreuil Wood in March 1918. Though casualties were high, Warrior escaped injury and was, too, awarded the Dickin Medal. The second great horse, Shergar, had a more unsettling story. He was a famous race horse and won many races including the Epsom Derby, Irish Derby, and Ascot races, all in 1981. To many he was a real-life equivalent to Pegasus, a winged horse from Greek mythology. With a unique white mark on his face and four white 'socks', he apparently ran "with his tongue lolling out of his mouth" (The Telegraph). But unfortunately on 8th February 1983 he was stolen from his stable by masked gunmen, never to be seen again. What actually happened to Shergar? Nobody knows for sure.

I cannot end on such a sad note, so I have added one more animal, actually a dinosaur, to the list: Dippy. He is a plaster diplodocus that for many years graced the great entrance hall, Hintze Hall, at London's Natural History Museum. He was presented to the museum by the industrialist, Andrew Carnegie, in 1905. Dippy shot to fame after he was the star of the 1975 Disney film 'One of our Dinosaurs is Missing', which followed the antics of a dinosaur who 'escaped' from the museum. Starring Peter Ustinov and Helen Hayes (amongst others), the film uses a skilful combination of suspense and humour, and is a great family movie to watch if you get the chance. Dippy will be on tour at various locations around the British Isles from 2018 to 2020 if you want to say hello.

Play: Meet the Famous Animals from Britain

Characters

Dippy, a dinosaur
Guy, a gorilla
Goldie, a golden eagle
Eros, a wild snowy owl
Belinda, a Mexican red-kneed spider
Winnie, a black bear
Brumas & Pipaluk, polar bears
Jumbo, an elephant
Unsinkable Sam, a cat
Tirpitz, a pig
Gustav, a pigeon
Warrior, a horse
Shergar, a horse
zookeeper

Script

Dippy: Hello. I'm Dippy. Thank you for coming here today. I am a dinosaur. I live in the Natural History Museum. Let me introduce you to my friends...

Guy: Hello. I'm guy. I'm a gorilla. I am very big. I live in London Zoo. Everyone likes me. Would you like a banana? Ooo-ooo!

Goldie: Hello. I'm Goldie. I'm a golden eagle. I escaped from London Zoo. I live in Regent's Park. Squawk!

Eros: Hello. I'm Eros. I am a wild snowy owl. I got lost at sea, and some soldiers rescued me. Thank you! Twit-twoo!

Belinda: Hello. I'm Belinda. I am a Mexican red-kneed spider. Don't be afraid – I'm very friendly! *(no noise, but can 'spin' a web)*

Winnie: Hello. I'm Winnie. I am a black bear. Do you know Winnie the Pooh? He's my friend. Roar!

Brumas & Pipaluk: Hello. I'm Brumas. And I'm Pipaluk. We are polar bears. We are very strong. We like people – but as friends, not as dinner! Roar!

Jumbo: Hello. I'm Jumbo. I'm an elephant. I am very big. Would you like a ride on my back? Jump on! Trumpet!

Sam: Hello. I'm Unsinkable Sam. I am a cat. I live on a ship. But I float – I don't sink! Meow!

Tirpitz: Hello. I'm Tirpitz. I'm a pig. I also live on a ship. I am very heavy, but I can swim. Oink!

Gustav: Hello. I'm Gustav. I'm a pigeon. Write a letter or postcard and I will deliver it for you. Coo! Coo!

Warrior: Hello. I'm Warrior. I'm a horse. I like to fight battles, and I always win! Neigh!

Shergar: Hello, I'm Shergar. I am a race horse. I am very fast. I win races. But I disappeared. Where am I? Neigh!

Dippy: Hello again. Remember me? I'm Dippy. Thank you for coming here today.

Everyone: We love animals! We are the famous animals from Britain! Goodbye! *(everyone waves goodbye)*

(All actors take a bow)

Director's Corner

In this script, famous animals from Britain are introduced, along with appropriate animal noises. There is great scope for dressing up, and your children and teens will have great fun – it could even make a lesson in itself. The play works well with large classes, and you could have more than one of each animal, or you could add scenes such as a group of zookeepers chasing the eagle, for example. I tried to keep the sentences short and the language simple – probably more suitable for primary children than teens.

The Set
- ✓ *a sign reading 'zoo'*
- ✓ *strips of black paper to represent cages and enclosures*

Costumes and Props Box
- ✓ *various animal costumes and masks*
- ✓ *various props, eg. banana, toy ship, etc.*
- ✓ *zookeeper's costume (long coat, hat and net)*

Sound and Lighting
- ✓ *recordings of animal sounds*

Other Considerations
- ✓ *do not use real animals ;-)*
- ✓ *the theme is that all children love animals*

turn again

UPGRADE

Dick Whittington and his Cat

In Brief

One of the most well-known characters of British folklore is Dick Whittington. He famously overcame poverty and a third-class lifestyle to become the Lord Mayor of London. But it was not his intention – it was only when he tried to leave London that the church bells called him back with the iconic words "Turn again, Whittington, Lord Mayor of London". Incredibly, he kept his obedient cat, Boots, with him throughout the saga, and it was the cat's ability to catch mice and rats that helped a young Dick to his prestigious post.

Dick Whittington was born in the countryside and for the first years of his life was poor, hungry and knew nothing of the city. He came to hear tales of London where the streets were paved with gold. With gold? His curiosity got the better of him and he set off with his trusty cat, Boots, to find his fortune.

But London was not what he expected: overcrowded, dirty streets, with a lot of people who had no time for him. What's more, the streets were not paved with gold! He eventually found work in a shop, moving boxes and delivering parcels to rich people. The job did not pay well, and his cat was little help in his toils. So Dick decided to leave and go back to his village. He said farewell to the shopkeeper and made his way north, into the rolling hills above London. But then something strange happened: as Dick and Boots walked up the steep slopes of Highgate Hill he heard the bells of Bow Church ring. They appeared to call to him, speaking the words "Turn again Whittington, Lord Mayor of London".

Dick and Boots looked at each other. Could church bells really speak? Surely not. But Dick took this as a sign and returned to the city.

He was amazed to find the place filled with unfriendly rats that ate all the people's food and destroyed their houses. Boots, however, did not see the problem and happily ran around town catching all the rats. The King noticed this and asked whose cat it was. It was Dick's. The King was very pleased, and immediately gave Dick his own horse, lots of gold, and made him Lord Mayor of London. Dick was a very worthy Lord Mayor, building houses, a college and a library for the poor. The King, Dick, Boots and all the city people were very happy.

What evidence of Dick Whittington can we see today? Probably most familiar are the many pantomimes that take up his story, often with a lot of humour. These pantomimes have their roots in the nineteenth century when this style of performance became popular. In London the Whittington Stone stands at the foot of Highgate Hill (close to the modern Wittington Stone pub). Though the stone was erected in 1821, the cat atop it was only added in 1964. In the City of London is St. Michael Patenoster Royal Church where Dick is buried; a plaque and stained glass window commemorate him. On College Hill nearby, there is another, similar plaque. Unfortunately, the exact location of Dick's grave has been lost over the years.

The Whittington Hospital (with its own trusty cat) stands on Highgate Hill, and is reputed to be the spot where Dick 'turned again'. Outside London, Whittington Castle stands in the village of Whittington, Shropshire. It was fully renovated and a tearoom and visitor attraction added in 2007, and was opened that year by the Duke of Gloucester. So don't ever give up – "turn again" just like Dick and Boots, and with perseverance you can achieve what you like!

Play: Dick Wittington and his Cat

Characters

Dick Whittington
Boots (Dick's Cat)
Shop Owner
King
The Church Bells
Rats (unspoken part)

Setting

Medieval London, timber-framed houses and cobbled streets, with green hills in the far distance

Script

Dick: Come on, Boots, let's go and find our fortune in London.
Boots: Meow! London?
Dick: Yes, Boots – London. They say the streets are paved with gold.
Boots: Meow! Gold? Meow!

Dick: *(to shop owner)* We are tired. We are hungry. Do you have a place for us to stay?
Shop Owner: Tired? Hungry? A place to stay? You have to work for your food and bed. Work!
Dick: OK. What shall I do?
Shop Owner: Move these boxes! Sweep the floor! Deliver these heavy boxes to the other side of town! Do it! Now!

Dick: Yes, yes, yes… *(Dick moves the boxes, sweeps the floor, and delivers the heavy boxes to the other side of town)* Boots, will you help me?
Boots: Meow! I'm a cat. I can't help. Sorry!
Dick: How about rats? Can you catch some rats?
Boots: Meow! No, I'm sleepy. When are we going home?
Dick: Let's go now. London is hard work, and this shop owner pays very little money. *(they walk up into the green hills; they hear something…)*
Church Bells: Dick, Dick, listen. Don't go, don't go. Come back to London, you will be rich, come back to London, you will be famous, turn again Dick Wittington, Lord Mayor of London!
Dick: What? Did the church bells speak to me?
Boots: Meow! Yes, I think they did!
Dick: I will not give up! I will not leave London!
Church Bells: Turn again, Wittington, Lord Mayor of London!

Boots: Meow! Look, a fine house. A fine house with lots of rats. I can help. I can catch all the rats. *(Boots chases and catches all the rats)*
King: Look! All the rats are gone! Whose cat is this?
Dick: It is my cat, Your Majesty. My name is Dick.
King: Your cat is a very good cat. And you are a good boy, Dick. Please, stay here with your cat and keep the rats away!
Boots: Meow! Yes, thank you, King.
King: And you, Dick, will be my Lord Mayor of London.
Dick: Yes, thank you, King. *(the King presents Dick and Boots with fine clothes and horses and lots of gold; they are all happy)*
King: *(speaks to audience)* Maybe next time it will be your turn?!
Everybody: Hooray for the King! Hooray for Boots! Hooray for Dick Wittington, Lord Mayor of London! *(they all clap and cheer)*

(All actors take a bow)

Director's Corner

You can use one set for all the parts, maybe hills on the left, medieval houses on the right. The part of Boots could be played by a (suitably dressed) student, or a toy cat can be used with the spoken words voiced over – it depends how many people are at hand. The King could be sitting on a throne, and he can also give a 'horse' for Boots to ride, which could be quite humorous!

The Set
- ✓ *hills and woods*
- ✓ *medieval (timber-framed) buildings*

Costumes and Props Box
- ✓ *boxes*
- ✓ *broom*
- ✓ *toy rat(s)*
- ✓ *hand-bell(s)*
- ✓ *some gold coins*
- ✓ *King's crown and red robe (think 'curtains')*
- ✓ *Lord Mayor's hat and robe*
- ✓ *horses (large cardboard cut-outs)*

Sound and Lighting
- ✓ *church bells (represented by hand-bells?)*

Other considerations
- ✓ *do not use a real cat ;-)*
- ✓ *the moral is that, with perseverance, you can achieve anything you want*

fighting
DRAGON

A Tale of Two Dragons

In Brief

Dragons have a powerful meaning as they represent not only strength and power but also destruction. Taking their place in mythology are two important British dragons: the poisonous dragon that St. George killed, and the proud Welsh dragon. Let's take these two dragons in turn.

Saint George is the patron saint of England and St. George's Day is 23rd April. He is identified with the English ideals of honour, bravery and gallantry. We think of him as dressed in a white tunic with a red cross, upon his horse, spearing a dragon as he rescues a fair maiden. But this is a myth and very little is known about the man himself. The fact that he was not English has become blurred into mythology.

Nonetheless, he has a lot to do with English identity.

Saint George became a well-known name in 1483 with the printing of the book The Golden Legend which was an account of various saints' lives. In it there is a town called Silene in Libya, a sufficiently exotic location for a dragon to live. The story goes that the town had a lake in which a plague-bearing creature lived. He was a poisonous beast, and to try to appease him, locals fed him two sheep each day. However, they ran out of sheep and started to feed it their own people out of fear, chosen by lottery.

One day the lot fell on the King's daughter, Sabra. Of course the king did not like this and tried to bargain his way out of the situation. He offered the people all his gold, silver and treasure and half his kingdom to spare his daughter – but the people refused. Reluctantly the king dressed his daughter in bridal clothes and sent her to the lake to await her fate.

By chance Saint George was riding by and, hearing her story, vowed to help her. As the dragon reared out of the lake, George held up the sign of the cross and charged the dragon on horseback, giving it a mighty wound with his spear. Amazingly the dragon then followed the king's daughter around 'like a meek beast' on a leash.

The dragon was led back to Silene but the people there were frightened at the terrifying sight. George appealed to the locals saying that if they consented to becoming Christians he would slay the dragon before them. They agreed, converted to Christianity, and George obligingly slew the dragon before their very eyes. Some say there was a tremendous fight, with a roaring sound louder than thunder; George had to hide behind an enchanted orange tree to re-gain his strength then rushed at the dragon and pierced it under its wing. The beast fell dead.

Naturally, the king was very pleased and offered George his daughter's hand in marriage.

Another king, Edward III of England, was an enthusiastic supporter of the story of Saint George, and in 1348 chose him as a special patron of the Order of the Garter and dedicated the chapel at Windsor Castle in the saint's honour. It was around this time that the legend moved to the mainstream of English society and his flag – a red cross on a white background – was widely adopted. Edward III proclaimed Saint George as "the most invincible athlete of Christ, whose name and protection of the English nation invoke as that of their patron, especially in war".

The second famous dragon from Britain evokes similar national feeling and inspires cultural identity: the Welsh Dragon ("Y Ddraig Goch") – as symbolised on the Welsh flag. Interestingly, Wales is not represented on the UK's Union Flag but has its own flag consisting a red dragon on a green and white background. The dragon was first used as a symbol of Wales in AD 829 and became the proud and ancient battle standard of Celtic leaders such as King Arthur. As such it is claimed to be the oldest national flag still in use.

The tale of the Welsh dragon first appeared in a collection of eleven stories, the Mabinogion, in which a red (welsh) dragon fights an invading white (English) dragon. Lludd, the King of Britain, asked his wise brother Llefelys for advice. He told Lludd to dig a pit in the centre of Britain, fill it with mead and cover it with cloth. As expected the dragons drank the mead and fell asleep. Lludd imprisoned them in Dinas Emrys in Snowdonia where the dragons remained trapped for centuries.

After a long time, King Vortigern tried to build a castle on the site. However, every night the castle walls and foundations were demolished by unseen forces (we know it was the dragons). Vortigern consulted his advisors who told him to find an orphan boy and sacrifice him, allowing him to build his castle. He chose a boy (who was later to become Merlin) who on hearing he is to be sacrificed tells the King the story of the red and white dragons. The King was convinced and excavated the area which in turn released the two dragons. The red and white dragons continued their fight until the red dragon finally won.

Merlin tells the King that the white dragon symbolises the Saxons (English) and the red dragon symbolises the people of Vortigern (later to become the Welsh). The King was pleased by this, and Merlin's life was spared.

The Welsh dragon defeated the English dragon, and that's why the dragon is such a proud and revered symbol of Wales. That's also why the dragon is on the flag of Wales. The Welsh flag as we know it was first used at the Battle of Bosworth Field in 1485, when Henry Tudor defeated Richard III. The dragon motif was brought to England by the House of Tudor that held the English throne from 1485 until 1603. Henry VII (the first Tudor king) added the green and white stripes to the flag. It was not until 1807, however, that the dragon design was recognised by the British parliament.

Interestingly, the heraldic use of the dragon used to be common throughout Europe, though Wales is the only nation to keep the image on its national flag. Today the Welsh dragon continues to be a positive and proud symbol, and can commonly be seen atop castles and public buildings. The same can be said for Saint George's flag in England, though it has competition from its brother, the Union Flag.

Play: Saint George and the Dragon

Characters

St. George
Dragon
King & King's Daughter
People 12&3
Sheep 12&3

Setting

A mighty stone castle in medieval England, rocky mountains and dark forest in the background; St. George's flag flaps happily in the wind.

Script

Dragon: Roar! Roar! I am I poisonous dragon! I eat people! *(he breathes fire)* Roar! Roar!
People 12&3: *(they run across the stage)* Oh, no! The poisonous dragon! Run, run, run!
Dragon: Roar! Roar! *(the dragon exits; the people enter sheepishly)*
Person 1: Has it gone?
Person 2: I think so. What was it?
Person 3: I don't know.
Person 1: It was a poisonous dragon.
(the King enters to a fanfare; everyone bows)
King: Do not worry, common people! We can feed it sheep to keep it happy. It will not disturb us!
Dragon: *(enters)* Roar! Roar! I am hungry!
Person 1: Here, dragon, take this delicious sheep.

Sheep 1: Baaaaa!
Dragon: Yummy! Roar! Roar!
Person 2: Here, dragon, take this delicious sheep.
Sheep 2: Baaaaa!
Dragon: Yummy! Roar! Roar!
Person 3: Here, dragon, take this delicious sheep.
Sheep 3: Baaaaa!
Dragon: Yummy! Roar! Roar!
King: There are no more sheep. What can we do?
Dragon: King, I will eat your daughter! Roar!
King's Daughter: Oh, no! Daddy! I don't want to be the dragon's dinner!
King: What can we do? Whoever kills the dragon can have my daughter's hand in marriage!
(suddenly St. George jumps onto stage, sword in hand)
George: Haha! I'm Saint George. Do not worry. I will kill the dragon. I will marry your daughter.
(he chases the dragon around the set, accompanied by much sword-waving and roaring; George hides behind an orange tree)
George: I will hide behind this enchanted orange tree, and surprise the dragon! *(he suddenly jumps out)* Haha! I have my mighty sword! It has the strength of 1,000 men! Take this, dragon! *(he spears the dragon with his sword).*
Dragon: Oh, no! I am dead! Roar! *(he falls; everyone claps and cheers)*
King: Well done, George. You killed the dragon. Here is my daughter. You can marry.
King's Daughter: Oh, George. I love you! *(she hugs George)*
George: Haha! The poisonous dragon is dead, and the King's daughter is mine!
Everybody: Hooray! *(they clap and cheer).*

(All actors take a bow)

Director's Corner

The special effects department can go to town on this one, especially sound effects such as the dragon's roar. The set need not be too complex – just a suggestion of castle-tops, mountains, and forest will do. Make sure your main characters (ie. George and the dragon) are suitably dressed – all other costumes can be very simple.

The Set
- ✓ castle walls
- ✓ cardboard mountains / forest
- ✓ St. George's flag (the red cross)

Costumes and Props Box
- ✓ dragon (green clothes and face mask)
- ✓ George's costume (white clothes with red cross)
- ✓ George's (cardboard) sword
- ✓ King & daughter's costumes: robes (old curtains), paper crowns
- ✓ sheep (white clothes and face mask)
- ✓ people's clothes (think 'charity shop')

Sound and Lighting
- ✓ recording of a dragon's (or lion's) roar
- ✓ recording of a sheep's bleat
- ✓ recording of a fanfare
- ✓ dragon's fire (torch or flashlight)

Other Considerations
- ✓ do not use real fire ;-)
- ✓ the moral is that with perseverance, all bad things can be defeated

SPLASH!

Looking For Nessie

In Brief

If we are to believe the various photos, films, sonar records and sightings then there really is a dinosaur-style monster in the depths of Loch Ness. The Cambridge Online Dictionary defines a monster as "an imaginary frightening creature, especially one that is large and strange".

Our 'monster' is called Nessie and belongs to a family known as cryptid with a sub-grouping as a lake monster. Accounts typically put the monster as between four to nine metres long, with one claim at thirty metres long. Commonly the animal has a small head, though there have been sightings of a large flat head and neck four or five metres long, or even a horned gargoyle head. Some describe the body as large and thick or even lumpy; protrusions at the bottom of the creature's body could be flippers or legs. Two or three humps have been seen to rise out of the water, the largest of which is around fifty feet in length. Its three metre tail is flattened and highly flexible. The animal can walk aswell as swim, crossing roads in front of drivers and onlookers, lurching like a seal. It has also been variously likened to an otter, a giant marine worm, an eel, or an elephant squid (complete with trunk and eye), and most often plesiosaur-like.

Its movement involves splashing and diving, turbulent swishing of its tail surrounded in a flurry of bubbles, rolling and plunging in the water like 'two fighting ducks'. It can move fast like a speedboat, sometimes with long bursts of movement, apparently.

Nessie is often spoken of as a solitary animal, but if it exists there must be at least two of them, or more likely a family of them.

Modern interest skyrocketed in the 1930s with a number of famous sightings and photographs, and since that time a whole stream of evidence has come forward. How we interpret this is up to us, but the wealth of evidence does seem to suggest the existence of some sort of creature. Looking at the modern sightings (since 1933) we can examine the evidence for and against the existence of the monster with the primary question: is the Loch Ness Monster real or fake?

Real: the evidence:

The sheer number of sightings is surely evidence enough, some of them quite by chance and others the result of expeditions and scientific study.

The most convincing photograph was taken on 19th April 1934 by Robert Kenneth Wilson, a London doctor, in what has become known as the 'Surgeon's Photograph'. He was foul shooting in the Highlands with a friend when they noticed a 'considerable commotion' in the water about 200 yards away. Wilson's friend shouted "my god, it's the monster!", and Wilson himself had time to take just four photos before it disappeared back into the water. Only two of the photos came out which he sold to the Daily Mail. One of the two photos became the iconic 'neck and head' photo. It is widely regarded as good evidence of the existence of the monster, and is a classic case of an eyewitness report being backed up with documentary proof.

Other evidence includes Stuart's 1951 'hump' photo and Edwards's 2011 photo; cine camera and video evidence includes Dinsdale 1960 and Holmes 2007; sonar evidence provided by Operation Deepscan in 1987; and Apple Maps 2014 satellite evidence of a 'mysterious shape' with a 'shadowy form' reported in the Daily Mail, the most recent evidence.

Fake: the evidence:

Sceptics have a lot of ammunition at their disposal, and it is easy to see their side of the story.

Many of the sightings have turned out to be hoaxes. Some claim the Surgeon's Photo of 1934 to be an elaborate fake. The scale of the photo is put into question, as it is often cropped to make the monster seem larger and the waves surrounding it disproportionately large. In the original image it is clear the water is in ripples, not large waves. The documentary Loch Ness Discovered (1993) found a man-made 'object', 60-90 cm long, to be the cause of the ripples as it was towed across the loch. Surgeon's photo was proved a fake in an article in The Sunday Telegraph in December 1975, and details emerged in 1999 about how the 'monster' was actually an adapted toy submarine bought from Woolworth's!

This lack of conclusive evidence is backed up by the BBC's 2003 study Searching for the Loch Ness Monster that failed to find any animal of any size (other than small fish and ducks) despite the use of sonar beams and satellite tracking. The study searched "from shoreline to shoreline, top to bottom" and concluded that Nessie is "only a myth".

There is a lot of debate about misidentification, as what people have seen might actually have been examples of animals that normally live in the habitat. 'Ducks fighting' has been mentioned above, but a more interesting suggestion is that Nessie is in fact a giant conger eel or cat-fish: they can grow to great sizes, especially in length, and can appear to look as sea serpents in the right light. Long-necked Seals are another explanation, and are also known to live in the loch. Though elephants are not normal in the habitat, they have been put forward as a possible explanation. Power and Johnson (1979) claimed that the Surgeon's photo was actually a swimming elephant, and that there were elephants in the loch from a travelling circus.

One final explanation for the sightings are inanimate objects such as trees and logs – Burton (1982) claimed that the shape of logs resembled descriptions of the monster, for example. Even with this considered, many descriptions are vague: a 'dark object' of 'considerable size', a 'murky form' or even just 'a shape in the water'.

Online there is countless information on Loch Ness and the history of expeditions and sightings. The sites specifically designed for use by primary children are particularly good. If you are lucky enough to travel to the Loch then the hotels and restaurants in the area are well versed in Nessie information and the needs of Nessie-hunters and offer a range of guidebooks, maps, and colouring books for children, and can organise a boat tour for a moderate fee. Evidently the existence of a monster is good for business.

What do you think? Is Nessie real or fake? Would you like to go on a 'monster expedition' to find Nessie?

Play: Looking For Nessie

Characters

Nessie
Boy and Girl
Doctor

Setting

Loch Ness, Scotland: green mountains drop to a murky lake.

Script

Nessie: Hello, I'm Nessie, and I live in Loch Ness. But nobody can find me. (he slips away; later…)

Boy: Hello. We are looking for Nessie.

Girl: We think he is friendly.

Boy: We think he is cute.

Girl: But where is he?

Nessie: *(briefly appears)* They look here, they look there, they cannot find me anywhere.

Doctor: I can help you find him. I have a special underwater camera. I have special sonar equipment.

Girl: Really?

Doctor: Of course. Let's go to the lake, and let's begin. First, let's try the underwater camera. *(he puts the camera into the lake).* You can see on this small screen.

Boy: I can't see anything.

Girl: Neither can I.

Doctor: Oh, dear, where is he?

Nessie: *(briefly appears)* They look here, they look there, they cannot find me anywhere.

Doctor: Let's try the sonar equipment. It looks for objects in the water.

Girl: Wow!

Boy: Really?

(the Doctor puts the sonar equipment into the water)

Doctor: Listen for the beeps. *(they wait)*

Boy: I can't hear anything.

Girl: Neither can I.

Doctor: Oh, dear, where is he?

Nessie: *(briefly appears)* They look here, they look there, they cannot find me anywhere.

Doctor: OK. One last chance. This is my special machine: a 'Nessie-Locator'. *(he reveals a strange looking machine)*

Girl: A 'Nessie-Locator'?

Doctor: A 'Nessie-Locator'.

Boy: A 'Nessie-Locator'?

Doctor: Yes, a 'Nessie-Locator'.

(the boy and girl look at each other in bewilderment)

Girl: But does it work?

Boy: Yes, does it work?

Doctor: Of course. I just turn these dials… and press this button… and the machine will find Nessie! *(he turns the dials, and presses the button… but the machine flies away into the distance)*

Boy: That didn't work!

Girl: No, we're never going to find Nessie!

Doctor: Yes, he is very difficult to find!

Nessie: They look here, they look there, they cannot find me anywhere. *(he laughs and disappears into the murky water, never to be found).*

(All actors take a bow)

Director's Corner

The set is very simple: just some rocky mountains and the suggestion of deep, murky water. Your main challenge is to dress your monster convincingly; it may take a lesson just to design a suitable costume! I'd recommend green clothes to start (T-shirt and track-suit bottoms) onto which you can add scales, wings, a tail, or whatever else that you like. You could also spend some time designing the doctor's equipment, especially the 'Nessie-Locator' with its buttons and dials.

The Set
- *green, rocky mountains*
- *dark, murky water*

Costumes and Props Box
- *doctor's coat and stethoscope*
- *underwater camera (with a small screen)*
- *sonar equipment*
- *'Nessie-Locator' with buttons and dials*

Sound and Lighting
- *recording of a monster's (lion's) roar*
- *the doctor's equipment could have flashing lights (such as Christmas tree lights)*

Other Considerations
- *do not use real water ;-)*
- *the moral is that some things are elusive, no matter how hard you look for them*

FAB
Super

The Beatles

In Brief

By far the biggest phenomenon in the western world during the 1960s was The Beatles, a hugely popular rock / pop group from Liverpool, England. Only those lucky enough to be standing in The Cavern Club in the early days could possibly imagine what was to come: a string of number one hit records, world tours, screaming fans, and their masterpiece album 'Sgt. Pepper's Lonely Hearts Club Band' (1967). Though I was born in 1970 – the same year that The Beatles split up – there was still enough of their magic around while I was growing up to soak in the feel of the era. It was an era of rock n' roll, experimentation, and unparalleled freedom of expression.

John Lennon met Paul McCartney in 1956 and they immediately became best friends. Both had a passion for music and formed their first band, The Quarry Men, in 1957. Their next band, The Beatles, was often found playing at the Cavern Club in Liverpool. Lennon and McCartney were soon joined by George Harrison and Ringo Starr.

After being turned down by Decca, The Beatles signed with a little-known British record company, Parlophone. Their first success in Liverpool and the north-east was as a backing group for Tony Sheridan, 'My Bonnie' (recorded 1961). This was soon followed by 'Love Me Do' (1962) which went to number 17 in the UK. By this time they had struck up a healthy working relationship with their producer, George Martin, and manager, Brian Epstein. They really hit the big time in 1963 with 'Please Please Me' and 'She Loves You' that went to number 2 and 1 in the UK respectively. In 1964 they went to number 1 in the USA with 'I Want to Hold Your Hand' and never looked back.

By 1964 the world was under the influence of 'Beatlemania': groups of screaming girls and fans followed the four around in a state of mania. This was epitomised in the film 'A Hard Day's Night' which had scenes of screaming, as adoring fans chased The Beatles through the streets of London. Though the film did not have a plot, it followed a day in the life of The Beatles as they travelled to a TV show. The film's director, Richard Lester, said that "the film wrote itself right in front of our eyes". In the shops you could buy Beatle dolls, books, mugs and all manner of souvenirs – or you might be lucky enough to go to a concert – if you could hear the music above the screaming!

A second memorable moment was the production of their masterpiece album, 'Sgt. Pepper's Lonely Hearts Club Band' in 1967. The four had disappeared from public view for quite some time in 1966 and 1967, and press and public alike wondered what had happened. Rumours abounded of a fantastic new album they were working on and, indeed, on 26th May 1967 the rumours were proved correct and the album was released. It was acclaimed as a masterpiece, the transition of pop into high art. Though only around 40 minutes long, the range of styles and complex quality of the songs was (and remains) unheard of. Take a listen if you get the chance.

I'll highlight a third memorable moment – The Beatles final live performance on the rooftop of their office buildings, Apple Corps, in London. By this time, 1969, the four were becoming tired of each other and of performing, so they agreed to do one last live concert but not in a stadium – on the office roof. Though there is clear tension evident, there is also much of the old enthusiasm and cheer of the early days. The humour came mostly from John Lennon who ended the concert with the legendary words "I'd like to say thank you on behalf of the group and ourselves, and I hope we passed the audition".

Play: When Lennon Met McCartney

Characters

John, Paul, George & Ringo
Manager
Fans

Setting

Various, including The Cavern Club in Liverpool, the USA, and Abbey Road Studios, London

Script

Scene 1: The Cavern Club, Liverpool

John, Paul, George & Ringo: La, la, la, la, love me do… La, la, la, la, she loves you… La, la, la, la, yeah, yeah, yeah…
Fans: Yeah!!! Woahhhhh!!! *(fans clap and scream)*

Scene 2: London in the early sixties

Manager: Welcome to London.
John: Thanks, man.
Paul: Yeah, it's great.
George: It's fab.
Manager: And what do you think, Ringo?
Ringo: I don't like your tie.

Scene 3: Beatlemania in the USA

Fans: We love you! Yeah!!! Woahhhhh!!! *(fans scream and scream and scream)*

John: How are we going to play our music?
Paul: I don't know. The fans are so noisy.
George: It's like Piccadilly Circus.
Manager: And what do you think, Ringo?
Ringo: I'm tired. I need a haircut.
(fans scream and shout)

Scene 4: Abbey Road Studios, London

Manager: We have to make a great music album.
John: Yeah, man. It has to be the best. *(he smokes a cigarette)*
Paul: We could do that Sgt. Pepper thing. It sounds fab. *(he smokes a cigarette)*
George: Yeah, it's fab. *(he smokes a cigarette)*
Manager: And what do you think, Ringo?
Ringo: Oh, I get by with a little help from my friends. *(he smokes a cigarette)*

Scene 5: Apple Corps roof, London

Fans: Yeah!!! Woahhhhh!!!
Paul: Get back, get back, get back...
John: Don't let me down, don't let me down...
George: Here comes the sun, diddle-oo-doo...
Ringo: I'd like to be, under the sea...
(all four perform an ad hoc jamming session, as fans scream and shout, and the manager looks on)
John: I'd like to say thank you on behalf of the group and ourselves, and I hope we passed the audition.
(everyone gives a short laugh, and claps)

(All actors take a bow)

Director's Corner

In the script above I attempt to capture the spirit of the Beatles' age (and I conveniently gloss over their messy break-up). You can phase from scene to scene with the fans clapping, screaming and shouting; scenes can also be delineated by change of costume / hairstyle, or musical interludes.

The Set
- ✓ *silhouettes of musical instruments*

Costumes and Props Box
- ✓ *guitars (toys, or made from cardboard)*
- ✓ *drum (baked bean can or bucket)*
- ✓ *'Beatle' wigs – crepe paper cut into strips and fastened at the top, or mop heads*
- ✓ *cigarettes – pencils or sticks*
- ✓ *colourful tie – from the charity shop*
- ✓ *fake moustaches – made from thick black paper*
- ✓ *thick outdoor coats (for the scene on Apple Corps roof) – just use your own coats*
- ✓ *long hair 'Beatle' wigs – again, think crepe paper*

Sound and Lighting
- ✓ *only use extracts from songs to avoid copyright issues*
- ✓ *stage-lights (torches) around the stage*

Other Considerations
- ✓ *you can use real Beatles – if you can find them!*
- ✓ *the moral is that working together can produce better results*

ART
GOLD

Winning the Eurovision Song Contest

In Brief

The first contest was held in 1956 with the aim of fostering greater partnership between European nations. The United Kingdom has won five times, with perhaps the biggest success being Buck's Fizz in 1981. With song titles such as 'Boom-Bang-A-Bang' and 'La-La-La', and competitors' questionable dress sense, the contest has become a bit of a joke in recent years, and the title of 'winner' is not necessarily a good one. If you win, it also means you have the burden of hosting the contest the following year which, for some poorer countries, does not in the least equate to 'winning'!

Ireland has won the contest the most times – seven. The United Kingdom has the dubious honour of having come second the most number of times - fifteen. The 'Big Five' countries (France, Germany, Spain, the UK, and Italy) contribute most money to the contest and therefore qualify automatically. All qualifying countries are European except one 'guest', Australia, whose presence in the 2015 contest was so popular that they have now been invited to be a permanent member.

OK, it's time for a quick run-down of UK winners, five in all, including 1969 when Lulu had to share the top spot with three other acts.

Sandie Shaw won the contest in 1967 with 'Puppet on a String'. It was a hugely popular song, especially in continental Europe where it achieved the number one slot in six countries. In the UK it remained at number one for three weeks. Despite its popularity, Sandie did not actually like the song, declaring that it was a "cuckoo-clock tune" that she hated "from the very first oompah to the final bang".

The UK's second success came two years later in 1969 with 'Boom-Bang-A-Bang' sung by Lulu. It was not alone in the top spot, however, sharing the trophy with three other entrants. It reached number 2 in the UK, and scored well in other countries. Lulu's song has gone down in Eurovision history as an early example of the 'dumbed-down' and jokey satirical attitude that has come to ghost the contest ever since. Monty Python had perhaps the most memorable parody in the shape of 'Bing-Tiddle-Tiddle-Bong' (1969).

1976 produced the next hit, 'Save Your Kisses for Me' by Brotherhood of Man. The quad of singers, two men and two women, has since become a trademark of the contest (see 1891 below, for example). The song remained at the UK number 1 spot for six weeks, and is one of the best-selling Eurovision songs ever. It went to number one in no less than 8 other countries, including Ireland, France, Spain, and the US Easy Listening Chart.

The UK did not have to wait long for its next success, 'Making Your Mind Up' by Buck's Fizz (1981). It is considered a classic Eurovision song and is generally held in high regard. Again the song was hugely popular, staying at number one for three weeks in the UK, and number one in Austria, Belgium and The Netherlands, amongst others. The song's 'clean disco' style was its selling point, as the four cheery singers paraded and jiggled about the stage in bright costumes (reinforcing the contest's tacky 'any idiot can understand it' image). It remains the UK's biggest success to date.

The fifth (and to date last) success came in 1997 with 'Love Shine a Light' by Katrina and the Waves. The song was a great commercial success, reaching number three in the UK and number two in Austria and Norway. It was originally written for the Samaritans charity, a representative of whom called it 'the kind of song that would win the Eurovision Song Contest' – and so it was entered at the last minute. The only slight controversy was that the band had already had chart success both in the UK and in Europe (eg. 'Walking on Sunshine'), but most agreed that the sheer quality of the production outweighed this negative. As Katrina herself later remarked: "It was such a feel-good, lighters-in-the-air, cheesy number... it had 'I am a winner' written all over it".

The five UK winners at least can boast that their tunes were worthy of the title – as compared to the usual Euro-trash affairs. When will the United Kingdom win again? Who knows. This year, 2017, the contest will be held (was held, by the time you read this) on Saturday May 13th at the International Exhibition Centre in Kiev, Ukraine. But don't hold your breath – of what I've seen from the sneak previews, we can expect the usual mix of jazzy costumes, painfully smiling faces, key changes, and unpredictable scoreboards, as ever.

UK EUROVISION WINNERS

Year	Song Title	Artist
1967	*Puppet On A String*	*Sandie Shaw*
1969	*Boom Bang-A-Bang*	*Lulu*
1976	*Save Your Kisses For Me*	*Brotherhood of Man*
1981	*Making Your Mind Up*	*Bucks Fizz*
1997	*Love Shine A Light*	*Katrina and the Waves*

UK EUROVISION No. 2's

Year	Song Title	Artist
1959	*Sing Little Birdie*	*Pearl Carr & Teddy Johnson*
1960	*Looking High, High, High*	*Bryan Johnson*
1961	*Are You Sure?*	*The Allisons*
1964	*I Love the Little Things*	*Matt Monro*
1965	*I Belong*	*Kathy Kirby*
1968	*Congratulations*	*Cliff Richard*
1970	*Knock, Knock (Who's There?)*	*Mary Hopkin*
1972	*Beg, Steal Or Borrow*	*New Seekers*
1975	*Let Me Be The One*	*The Shadows*
1977	*Rock Bottom*	*Lynsey de Paul & Mike Moran*
1988	*Go*	*Scott Fitzgerald*
1989	*Why Do I Always Get It Wrong?*	*Live Report*
1992	*One Step Out Of Time*	*Michael Ball*
1993	*Better The Devil You Know*	*Sonia*
1998	*Where Are You?*	*Imaani*

Play: Winning the Eurovision Song Contest

Characters

Sandie Shaw
Lulu
Martin
Nicky
Sandra
Lee
Bobby
Mike
Jay
Cheryl
Katrina
The Waves
Host
Judges 12&3

Setting

A gaudy and glitzy stage somewhere in Continental Europe.

Script

Scene 1: 1967 (Sandie Shaw) & 1969 (Lulu)

Host: Ladies and gentlemen, boys and girls, welcome to the Eurovision Song Contest! Let's have our first act!
(everyone claps and cheers)

Sandie: Hi, I'm Sandie Shaw, and I won the Eurovision Song Contest in 1967 with the song 'Puppet on a String'.
Lulu: And I'm Lulu. I won the contest in 1969 with 'Boom-bang-a-bang'.
Sandie: *(she sings) Like a puppet on a string…*
Lulu: *(she sings) Boom-bang-a-bang…*
Host: Ladies, ladies! Let's see what the judges think.
Judges: *(holding up their scorecards)* Twelve points!
(everyone claps and cheers)

Scene 2: 1976 (Brotherhood of Man)

Host: And now let's have our next act!
(everyone claps and cheers)
Martin: Hi, I'm Martin.
Nicky: Hi, I'm Nicky.
Sandra: Hi, I'm Sandra.
Lee: Hi, I'm Lee.
Altogether: And we're Brotherhood of Man. We won the Eurovision Song Contest in 1976. *(they sing and dance motionless and sad) Kisses for me, save all your kisses for me…*
Host: Hold on, hold on!
Altogether: What?
Host: You're not moving. You have to move and be happy. Move! Be happy!
Martin: You mean like this? *(dances happily and smiles)*
Nicky: And this? *(dances happily and smiles)*
Sandra: And this? *(dances happily and smiles)*
Lee: And this? (dances happily and smiles)
Host: Yes, that's better. Now try again.
Martin: Hi, I'm Martin.
Nicky: Hi, I'm Nicky.
Sandra: Hi, I'm Sandra.

Lee: Hi, I'm Lee.
Altogether: And we're Brotherhood of Man! *(they sing) Kisses for me, save all your kisses for me...*
Host: OK. Let's see what the judges think.
Judges: *(holding up their scorecards)* Twelve points!
(everyone claps and cheers)

Scene 3: 1981 (Buck's Fizz)

Host: And now let's have our next act!
(everyone claps and cheers)
Bobby: Hi, I'm Bobby.
Jay: Hi, I'm Jay.
Mike: Hi, I'm Mike.
Cheryl: Hi, I'm Cheryl.
Altogether: And we're Bucks Fizz! We won the Eurovision Song Contest in 1981. *(they sing) You gotta speed it up, you gotta slow it down...*
Host: Hold on, hold on!
Altogether: What?
Host: You're wearing the wrong clothes. Don't wear black. Wear colourful colours!
Bobby: You mean like this? *(rips off black top to reveal colourful T-shirt)*
Jay: And this? *(rips off black top to reveal colourful T-shirt)*
Mike: And this? *(rips off black top to reveal colourful T-shirt)*
Cheryl: And this? *(rips off black top to reveal colourful T-shirt)*
Host: Yes, that's better. Now try again.
Bobby: Hi, I'm Bobby.
Jay: Hi, I'm Jay.
Mike: Hi, I'm Mike.
Cheryl: Hi, I'm Cheryl.
Altogether: And we're Bucks Fizz! *(they sing) You gotta speed it up, you gotta slow it down...*

Host: Let's see what the judges think.
Judges: *(holding up their scorecards)* twelve points!
(everyone claps and cheers)

Scene 4: 1997 (Katrina and the Waves)

Host: And now let's have our final act!
(everyone claps and cheers)
Katrina: Hi, I'm Katrina.
The Waves: Hi, and we're the Waves.
Altogether: And We're Katrina and the Waves. *(they sing and wave their arms in the air) Love shine a light…*
Host: Hold on, hold on!
Altogether: What?
Host: Your hair is wrong. You have boring hair! Make your hairstyle crazy!
Katrina: You mean like this? *(puts on crazy hair)*
The Waves: And this? *(put on crazy hair)*
Host: Yes, that's better. Now try again.
Katrina: Hi, I'm Katrina.
The Waves: Hi, and we're the waves.
Altogether: And we're Katrina and the Waves. *(they sing and wave their arms in the air) Love shine a light…*
Host: Let's see what the judges think.
Judges: *(holding up their scorecards)* Twelve points!
(everyone claps and cheers, then all actors leave the stage except the Host and the Judges; they shake their heads…)
Host: What a bunch of losers!
Judges: Yes, what a bunch of losers!

(All actors take a bow)

Director's Corner

Get your glitterball and sparkly costumes ready: you can really go to town on this one. Use just one set for the entire performance, and make sure your props table is well laid-out and within easy reach. It's very suitable for a large class because of the many characters (I counted at least sixteen), with each group practicing their part separately at first. Whether you source the songs and play extracts from them is up to you – but if they are used, make sure you have a good technical director!

The Set
- ✓ *a sparkly backdrop*
- ✓ *a table and three chairs for the judges*

Costumes and Props Box
- ✓ *top hat and jacket for the host*
- ✓ *sparkly costumes*
- ✓ *black T-shirts for Buck's Fizz*
- ✓ *various wigs (think strips of crepe paper fastened at the top)*
- ✓ *judges' scorecards (×3)*
- ✓ *a trophy (the same one can be used for all contestants)*

Sound and Lighting
- ✓ *recordings of the original songs (extracts only)*
- ✓ *stage lighting (to shine on the sparkly backdrop)*
- ✓ *spotlight*

Other Considerations
- ✓ *only use extracts of original songs to avoid copyright issues*
- ✓ *ear plugs are very handy*

celebrity

A Visit to Madame Tussauds

In Brief

Have you ever met Her Majesty the Queen, the President of the USA, or famous sports stars like Sebastian Coe or Ronaldo? Your chance is here at Madame Tussauds Waxworks Museum.

Famous people – in wax – lurk around every twist and corner, and appear real and life-like before your very eyes. They are grouped according to theme, such as 'world leaders', 'party', 'film', 'sports', or 'royals'. In each section visitors have the opportunity to have their photo taken with the famous, and brag to their friends when they get home that they actually mixed with the stars.

The waxworks museum has a long and proud history, spanning over 250 years. Madame Tussaud herself was born in 1761 in Strasbourg, and first produced a wax figure, of the famous author and philosopher Francois Voltaire, in 1777. During the French Revolution she was imprisoned at Laforce Prison, Paris, and was only released on condition that she made death masks for the executed royals and nobles. At the end of the Revolution she inherited a large wax collection. In 1795 she married Francois Tussaud, giving her her name. In 1802 she took the exhibition on tour in the British Isles and established a base in London in 1835.

After her death in 1850, her grandsons moved the attraction to its current location on Marylebone Road. But there were two unfortunate events that followed: in 1925 the museum was devastated by fire (but restored and re-opened in 1928); and in 1940 the building was hit by a bomb, destroying much of the site. Since restoration, the exhibition has become a worldwide success: there are currently eighteen Madame

Tussauds' around the world, including Las Vegas, New York, Hong Kong, Sydney and Tokyo. 2011 saw the 250-year anniversary of the museum.

These days visitors can stroll through a number of zones at their leisure. In the 'world leaders' section you can see Donald Trump and Nelson Mandela. In the 'party' section you can rub shoulders with David and Victoria Beckham, whilst in the 'film' studio you can meet Whoopi Goldberg and Leonardo DiCaprio. There are sports stars galore including Rafael Nadal and Cristiano Ronaldo; royals such as Queen Elizabeth II and Prince Harry; cultural and scientific figures like Shakespeare or Einstein; music stars like Michael Jackson and One Direction; and fictional characters such as Spiderman or BB8.

In additional to the traditional displays, there are some interactive attractions such as entering the Big Brother diary room, or taking a penalty shot alongside David Beckham. The latest attraction (as of Spring 2017) is 'KONG', the giant gorilla, which dares the visitor to go face-to-face with the fearsome beast. Don't forget - all this is presented to us in glorious wax!

Critical reception has of late been mixed: a glance at one of the popular holiday advisory web sites demonstrates this. Whilst some visitors (as of spring 2017) call it a 'great' or 'funny' experience that is 'worth it', others bemoan the 'long' and 'chaotic' queues. The same site ranks Madame Tussauds as number 101 of nearly 1,600 things to do in London. My opinion is that it is good if you can find a way to beat the queues – buy your tickets in advance and opt for an early slot, for instance.

So why do we love gawping and mixing with these wax statues? As the Madame Tussauds website itself suggests, it's all because of "good old-fashioned curiosity".

Play: A Visit to Madame Tussauds

Characters

Boy & Girl
Donald Trump
Michael Jackson
Phil Collins
Ronaldo
Queen Elizabeth
Ticket Inspector

Setting

Madame Tussauds Waxworks Museum, London.

Script

Boy: Where shall we go? Hmmm... *(he thinks)*
Girl: I don't know... *(she thinks)*
Boy: I know. Let's go to Madame Tussauds!
Girl: Yeah, great idea!
Boy: Who will we see?
Girl: Let's go and find out...

Boy: Who are you?
Donald Trump: I'm Donald Trump. I've got lots of money. Bigly! *(he waves wads of money in the air)*
Girl: What do you do?

Donald Trump: I'm President of the USA. I love beautiful… *(he pauses briefly)* babies.

Boy: Who are you?
Michael Jackson: I'm Michael Jackson, *(sings) It don't matter if you're black or white*, oh!...
Girl: What do you do?
Michael Jackson: I'm a singer. I'm dead cool! Actually, I'm dead! Beat it!

Boy: Who are you?
Phil Collins: I'm Phil Collins. *(sings) I can feel it in the air tonight…*
Boy: Are you dead?
Phil Collins: No, I'm not dead yet.
Girl: What do you do?
Phil Collins: I'm a singer, *(sings) Just another day for you and me in paradise…*

Boy: Who are you?
Ronaldo: I'm Ronaldo. *(tries to spin a football on his finger)*
Girl: What do you do?
Ronaldo: I'm the best football player in the world! *(kicks his football about a bit)…*
Boy & Girl: Hmmm…

Boy: Who are you?
Queen Elizabeth: I'm Queen Elizabeth. I am *not* amused!
Girl: What do you do?
Queen Elizabeth: I sit on the throne and wear a crown.
Girl: Oh, really. But what do you do?
Queen Elizabeth: Hmmm… *(she thinks)* I open hospitals for little children, and give names to ships, and chop peoples' heads off. Off with his head! *(she waves a toy axe)*

Boy: Who are you? You must be someone really famous. Can I have your autograph?
Girl: Don't be silly, that's not anyone famous. That's the ticket inspector!
Ticket Inspector: Tickets, please!
(Boy, Girl & Ticket Inspector laugh)

(All actors take a bow)

Director's Corner

This is one of those scripts where groups can practice each part separately, then perform together at the end. Be creative with the costumes, as your children and teens will delight in dressing up as famous people – don't be afraid to go over the top. It's probably better to range the famous people around the stage and have the boy and girl walk to each one in turn. A spotlight might help focus the audience's attention, if you have one!

The Set
- ✓ *sparkly backdrop, with large stars*

Costumes and Props Box
- ✓ *New York baseball cap*
- ✓ *wad of (fake) money*
- ✓ *Michael Jackson costume*
- ✓ *'bald head' wig for Phil Collins*
- ✓ *football player's costume and football*
- ✓ *crown, red robe, and throne (a decorated chair)*
- ✓ *toy axe*
- ✓ *inspector's hat and jacket*

Sound and Lighting
- ✓ *torches, flashlights, or a spotlight for various lighting effects*
- ✓ *glitterball ?*
- ✓ *extracts of Michael Jackson and Phil Collins songs*

Other Considerations
- ✓ *don't use the full versions of songs because of copyright issues*
- ✓ *the moral is the fallacy ('fake-ness') of celebrity and fame*

MYSTERY
GUN

Sherlock Holmes

In Brief

When we think of famous detectives, we think of Agatha Christie's Miss Marple or Hercule Poirot; we think of Herge's Tintin; we think of Columbo; and we think of Jessica Fletcher in 'Murder She Wrote'. But perhaps the most famous detective of all time is Sir Arthur Conan Doyle's Sherlock Holmes.

None of these people actually existed, of course, except in our imaginations. Baker Street, however, is not imaginary – it is just around the corner from Madame Tussauds in London. It was here at number 221b that Sherlock lived with his companion, Doctor John H. Watson, from 1881 until 1904. His arch-rival, Professor Moriarty, was never far away. Holmes had the mysterious knack for solving crimes – mostly murders or theft of expensive jewellery – and had made a good name for himself. Victorian London could be a cold and corrupt place, rife with crime, murder, and wrong-doing.

Though those in polite society could generally insulate themselves from the worst of this, there were occasions when corrupt or dishonest characters made their bad influence felt to those of money or position. Holmes' greatest misfortune was the evil Professor Moriarty, whose presence in the stories was symbolic of the worst side of human nature.

You will no doubt be familiar with many of the icons of Holmes' character: his smoker's hat, his pipe, his magnifying glass; and that he would declare to a bemused Dr. Watson that solving a crime was "elementary, my dear Watson".

Sir Arthur Conan Doyle wrote his first Holmes story in 1886, and in total there were fifty-six official stories published from 1886 to 1927. The stories were enormously popular. Even when Holmes was killed off by his arch-rival Moriarty, there was such public clamour for more that the character was miraculously brought back to life. The most famous of the stories are 'A Study in Scarlet' (1886), 'The Sign of Four' (1890), and 'The Hound of the Baskervilles' (1902).

In *A Study in Scarlet* Watson meets Holmes for the first time. He becomes fascinated by Holmes, an eccentric with the unusual ability to reason backwards, following observation and deduction. The thrust of the novel is the murder of two men from America; Holmes is able to show that a London cab driver was the murderer.

In *The Sign of Four* Mary Morston visits Holmes and Watson at their apartment in Baker Street. Her story leads them to a tale about stolen and hidden treasure. Watson falls in love with Mary and proposes to her. The third novel *The Hound of the Baskervilles* is considered by many to be Doyle's best work. It is not set in London but rather Dartmoor in southern England: a sad, wild and desolate place, in which much of the action takes place.

There is a splendid Sherlock Holmes exhibition at 221b Baker Street, London, which includes a mock-up of his first floor study, and waxworks figures of him, Dr. Watson and Moriarty. Of course, it has a gift shop. You may want to take one of Conan Doyle's books with you, as the wait to get in can take some time (and leave a large hole in your pocket). Fans will agree that it is worth the pain!

Play: The Murder of Mrs. Custard

Characters

Sherlock Holmes
Dr. Watson
Mrs. Custard (the victim)
Mr. Pepper / Moriarty

Setting

Inside Holmes's apartment, and in Baker Street, London.

Script

Scene 1: Holmes's apartment, Baker Street

(Sherlock Holmes relaxes in his armchair, smoking his pipe)
Holmes: Oh, Watson, what's in the paper today?
Watson: Hmmm… nothing much. Just the usual economic problems, a new spaghetti factory, the train drivers have gone on strike again, you know, the usual. Hold on! Look, Mrs. Custard, the famous opera singer, has been murdered!
Holmes: I know.
Watson: You know? How could you possibly know?
Holmes: I know everything. *(he pauses briefly)* You see, it all happened a few weeks ago while you were away on business. The Lake District, wasn't it?
Watson: Actually, it was the Peak District.

Holmes: Right. The Peak District. Well, I was in the street one evening when… *(the scene fades)*

Scene 2: In Baker Street

Mrs. Custard: Sherlock Holmes? That is you, isn't it?
Holmes: It may be.
Mrs. Custard: Oh, please, Mr. Holmes, please help me. Someone is trying to kill me.
Holmes: Really? Why do you think that?
Mrs. Custard: I have a note. Look. *(she hands the note to Holmes)*
Holmes: *(he reads aloud)* "Mrs. Custard, you are a bad woman. I will kill you. P". Who is this 'P'?
Mrs. Custard: I don't know.
(suddenly…)
Mr Pepper: Haha! It is me, Mr Pepper! *(he is holding a revolver and points it at Mrs. Custard)*
Mrs. Custard: Oh, Mr. Pepper, what are you doing?
Mr. Pepper: I hate you! I will kill you!
Holmes: Wait, Mr. Pepper. Maybe I can help.
Mr. Pepper: No, you can't! *(he takes off his mask to reveal that he is actually Moriarty)*
Holmes: Moriarty? I should have known!
Mr Pepper: Haha! Yes, it is me, Moriarty! I don't want to kill *you*, Mrs. Custard, I want to kill *him (he points the gun at Holmes; there is a struggle and the gun goes off; a bullet hits Mrs. Custard)*
Mrs. Custard: Oh, no! I am shot! Ahhhhh! I am dead! *(she falls)*
Mr Pepper: next time it will be *YOU*, Sherlock Holmes! Haha! *(he laughs a terrible laugh, and disappears into the fog).*

Scene 3: Holmes's apartment, Baker Street

Watson: So it's true? You knew all along?
Holmes: Yes, Watson.
Watson: You were *there*, when Mrs. Custard, the famous opera singer, was murdered?
Holmes: Yes, Watson.
Watson: But how did you *know*?
Holmes: *(he relaxes and smokes his pipe)* I know everything. You see, Moriarty *pretended* to be Mr. Pepper. He wrote the note, and sent it to Mrs. Custard. He knew Mrs. Custard would bring the note to me and that, in turn, would lead Moriarty to me. (he looks down) He could then try *(he pauses and looks up)* to *kill* me. You see, it's elementary, my dear Watson.

(All actors take a bow)

Director's Corner

In terms of direction and set, this is a fairly easy one to stage, with only two locations, both very simple. Your biggest challenge is to get the struggle scene right, especially 'the shot'. Remember that Mr. Pepper is Professor Moriarty (Holmes's arch-rival) in disguise.

The Set
   ✓ *windows and a fireplace (cardboard)*
   ✓ *street lamps*

Costumes and Props Box
   ✓ *Holmes' armchair*
   ✓ *a toy revolver or water pistol*
   ✓ *newspaper*
   ✓ *the murder note*
   ✓ *Mr. Pepper's mask*
   ✓ *jackets for Holmes and Watson*
   ✓ *cape for Moriarty*
   ✓ *smoker's hat and pipe*

Sound and Lighting
   ✓ *a gunfire sound for 'the shot'*
   ✓ *an extract of an opera singer singing (female)*

Other Considerations
   ✓ *do not use a real gun ;-)*
   ✓ *the moral is that you never know who your friends and enemies are*

GHOST

Henry VIII and His Six Wives

In Brief

King Henry VIII is known for his succession of wives, some of whom met a deadly fate and return from time to time as ghosts.

Henry's favourite home was Hampton Court Palace in Surrey, and here he created a palace truly fit for a King. He held banquets here, sitting at the high table (one step above floor level) whilst his guests sat at tables ranged along the main walls.

Despite the fact that the palace was well-guarded, Henry was well aware of possible threats to the Crown and to himself. Each night a small army of servants prepared and searched his bed, probing the straw on which Henry's mattress lay with a dagger to ensure nothing was concealed; at mealtimes he had tasters to ensure his food was not poisoned. Apparently he could be generous if he liked someone but dangerous if he did not. This is something his six wives were to find out.

His greatest wish was to produce a son and heir, and this reason alone led to the failure of many of his marriages. He was married to his first wife, Katherine of Aragon, for twenty-four years, and they had a daughter (later Mary I). But Henry wanted a son, and so divorced her after she became too old to bear children.

He took Anne Boleyn as his mistress, then wife, and moved to Hampton Court with her and set about enlarging the palace: another gallery, library, study, kitchens, tennis court and wine cellar. They also produced a daughter (later Elizabeth I) which angered Henry who expected a son. This, together with her unlucky gambling, led to her beheading at the Tower of London on 19th May 1536.

Soon after appeared Jane Seymour, for whom he furnished new apartments at Hampton Court. Only ten days after Anne's beheading he married Jane who, on 12th October 1537 gave birth to a son (later Edward VI). This, of course, made Henry very happy, but his delight was short-lived as soon after Jane became very ill and her strength disappeared. Twelve days after the birth she died.

Henry married and divorced his sixth wife, Anne of Cleaves, very quickly. He had been told of the twenty-four year old's attractiveness, and so on New Year's Day 1540 he sailed down the Thames to Rochester to meet Anne and her ship. Unfortunately he did not like the look of his new bride-to-be, but the marriage contract was set in place. Days after their marriage their divorce was approved.

Later in 1540 he married wife number five, Catherine Howard, and at first the marriage went well. However, Henry increasingly felt that she had nothing much to offer him and, noting elicit sexual relations with other men, had her beheaded at the Tower on 10th February 1542.

His final wife was Kateryn Parr, aged thirty-one, who he married in 1543. By now Henry was in old age, and her affectionate and domestic manner was well suited to his age and temperament. She outlived him: Henry VIII died at Westminster Palace on 28th January 1547 with the famous words "All is lost!".

Do some of Henry VIII's wives still 'live' as ghosts? Apparently so. There have been several spooky sightings of Jane Seymour. A tall lady dressed in white with a long train and a smiling face is said to glide around Clock

Court, the Queen's Old Apartments and the Silver Stick Gallery. She has been said to pass through closed doors and glide up and down stairs.

After her grisly fate at the Tower in 1542, Catherine Howard has been sighted many times in the Haunted Gallery, named after her famous ghost. Henry had had her held in her room at the palace awaiting removal to the Tower. She managed to break free and run along the gallery in an effort to plead for her life with her husband. However Henry, who was celebrating mass in the chapel, paid no attention to her. She was held back by the guards who dragged her back to her room shrieking and sobbing for mercy. Her 'piercing scream' could be heard all over the palace.

The shadowy image of a woman in a white gown has been seen near the door to the royal pew in the chapel. The image vanishes suddenly to the sound of a blood-chilling scream. The shrieking figure runs through the Haunted Gallery on the night of the anniversary of her death. Residents in the palace's apartments have reported being awakened in the night by shrieks that seemed to come from the Haunted Gallery. The most recent sighting was in 1945 by a resident, Mr. Irwin. He saw a female in strange dress walking around the palace gardens at noon; a waiter who overheard his conversation remarked that Catherine had been "walking a great deal lately".

Finally, Anne Boleyn, another victim of beheading, was also reportedly seen in the Haunted Gallery in the late 1800s. Dressed in blue, she surprised a servant who recognised her from a portrait in the palace.

What do you make of all this? It may be an idea to go and look for yourself. Hampton Court is a very popular tourist destination with prices to match. The easiest way is to travel from London Waterloo to

Hampton Court station (about thirty minutes). From the station there is a pleasant walk across Hampton Court Bridge to the main entrance at Trophy Gate. From April to September there are also river boats from Westminster, Richmond and Kingston: fake paddle steamers in true Mississippi style.

The front and side gardens are free of charge, as are the rear gardens out of season. If you'd like to enter the palace itself then be prepared for an eye-watering charge to get in. There is no shortage of cafes, bars and restaurants in the area, especially around Bridge Road near the railway station. If you have a thin wallet then a packed lunch on the main lawn is a better option.

Play: Meet Henry VIII's Wives

Characters

King Henry VIII
Katherine of Aragon
Anne Boleyn
Jane Seymour
Anne of Cleves
Catherine Howard
Kateryn Parr
Doctor
axe-weilder

Setting

In the gardens at Hampton Court, the palace is in the background, to the left and right are formal trees, and there is a small fountain.

Script

Henry: Good day. My name is King Henry VIII and I live at Hampton Court Palace. I am a generous man but I can be dangerous too.

(thunder clap)

Henry: Oh my goodness! What is that?
Katherine of Aragon: It is me, your first wife, Katherine of Aragon. I was a good wife to you for over twenty years, and I gave you a daughter, Mary. But you divorced me!
Henry: But I don't want a daughter, I want a son. Be gone!

(thunder clap)

Henry: What? Again?
Anne Boleyn: Haha! I am Anne Boleyn, Henry's second wife. We had a daughter, Elizabeth, together. But I am angry. Why? Because you had me beheaded!
Henry: Off with her head!
Axe-wielder: I will cut off your head! *(cuts off head)*

(thunder clap)

Henry: Oh, no! Not another one!
Jane Seymour: Good day, it is me, Jane Seymour. I was Henry's third wife. I gave birth to a son, Edward. But I died in childbirth.

Henry: Oh, no! Jane is dead, but now I have a son. *(he thinks)* Hmmm, who shall I marry next?

(thunder clap)

Anne of Cleves: It shall be me, Anne of Cleves. I am from Germany. You must marry me.
Henry: Of, my goodness, she is so ugly! I will divorce you. Goodbye.

(thunder clap)

Catherine Howard: I am Catherine Howard, Henry's fifth wife.
Henry: Hmmm, you look nice…
Catherine Howard: I like you, Henry, but I like other men too.
Henry: Other men? But I am your husband! You are my wife! I am the king! Off with her head!
Axe-wielder: I will cut off your head! *(cuts off head)*

(thunder clap)

Henry: Another one?
Kateryn Parr: I am Henry's last wife, Kateryn Parr. Look! Henry is so old now. I will look after him. I will be with him when he dies.
Doctor: He is very old. He is going to die soon.
Henry: Now I am very sick. It's time to die. *(shrieks)* "All is lost".

(All actors take a bow)

Director's Corner

This can be a very dramatic script. The play introduces Henry VIII and his six wives in turn and it also has parts for an axe-wielder (usually a popular part) and a doctor. I had some problems with the tenses in this play, but decided that Henry should speak in the present, and his wives, as ghosts, should speak in the present and past. The set is very simple, but you can be more creative with costume and props.

The Set
- ✓ *backdrop of the formal gardens of Hampton Court Palace*

Costumes and Props Box
- ✓ *King's crown and robe*
- ✓ *the wives' costumes (think 'charity shop')*
- ✓ *a (toy) axe*
- ✓ *executor's block (cardboard box)*
- ✓ *doctor's white coat and stethoscope*

Sound and Lighting
- ✓ *recording of a thunderclap*
- ✓ *a loud shriek*

Other Considerations
- ✓ *do not use a real axe ;-)*
- ✓ *the moral is that your bad past can come back to haunt you – so be good!*

battle
HOORAY!

King Harold and the Battle of Hastings

In Brief

1066 is an important year in British history. It was the year King William of Normandy invaded, forcing a great battle near Hastings in southern England, and leading to the death of King Harold. Famously, Harold died when an arrow shot him in the eye. It was an event that marked the end of the Saxons and is widely viewed by historians as the start of Medieval Britain.

King Harold II was born in around 1020 in Wessex, and became the Earl of Wessex in 1053, making him the second most powerful man in England. He was crowned on January 6th 1066, and became one of the shortest reigning monarchs at just under ten months.

But there was a problem: William of Normandy (also known as William the Conqueror) claimed the English throne had been promised to him, and resented the coronation of Harold. William prepared to invade England to claim the throne. In October 1066 William and his army landed near Hastings, on the south-east English coast. They made their way steadily inland until they reached the area that is now known as Battle. The Battle of Hastings took place on 14th October 1066. William's soldiers were superior, and after fierce fighting led William to victory. Famously, King Harold died when an enemy arrow pierced his eye, a scene which is depicted in the Bayeux Tapestry in Bayeux, France.

On 10th December 1066 William entered London and declared himself King. Nobody was going to argue.

1066 was also the year Halley's Comet passed by the earth, and many saw this as an omen of Harold's fate. This is clearly depicted in the Bayeux Tapestry.

Other than going to look at the Bayeux Tapestry in Normandy, France, your best bet is the area around the seaside resort of Hastings. Hastings is a pleasant, if slightly ageing, seaside resort on the East Sussex coast. Visitors can view Hastings Castle high above the town, and a series of spooky caves within the rock below it. On the shingly beach are some interesting fisherman's huts and, of course, Hastings Pier.

To find evidence of the Battle of Hastings you have to travel inland to the pretty town of Battle. Battle Abbey is the most interesting attraction: a crumbly assortment of window-less arches and ruined walls, built around the location of the battle. Within the abbey there is a plaque before the High Altar: the place where King Harold fell. For me the location in a typically picturesque English landscape is enough, especially on a warm summer's day.

Play: King Harold and the Battle of Hastings

Characters

King Harold
King William of Normandy
Harold's Soldiers
William's Soldiers
farmers 1&2

Setting

Green rolling hills with one large oak tree, birds sing gently, cows graze.

Script

(two farmers lean against a tree)

Farmer 1: Ah, nice day, isn't it?
Farmer 2: Ah, yes it is.
Farmer 1: Nothing ever happens in this village, does it?
Farmer 2: Nah, nothing ever happens.
Farmer 1: It's so boring.
Farmer 2: That it is.
Farmer 1: How's your cow?
Farmer 2: She's fine, thank you...

(suddenly there is a loud battle cry and the sound of horse's hoofs)

William: Charge! Men and horses! Charge!
William's Soldiers: Charge!
Harold: What's that? Oh, no! Men! Charge!
Harold's Soldiers: Charge!
(the two groups of soldiers fight and battle)
William: Men! Use the arrows!
William's Soldiers: Arrows!
Harold: What's that? Oh, no! Arrows!
(Williams soldiers shoot their arrows)
Harold: What's that? Oh, no! I am hit! I have an arrow in my eye!
Ahhhhhh! I am dead! *(he dies, and all of his soldiers die)*
William: We win! Britain is ours!
William's Soldiers: Hooray! Hooray!

(meanwhile, back at their tree, the two farmers are still chatting)

Farmer 1: What was that? Did you hear something?
Farmer 2: No, I didn't.
Farmer 1: Nothing ever happens in this village, does it?
Farmer 2: Nah, nothing ever happens.
Farmer 1: How's your cow?
Farmer 2: Well, you see…
(the two farmers pretend to chat, as lights fade)

(All actors take a bow)

Director's Corner

With this script I really wanted to highlight the difference between the lowly peasant farmers, in tune with the trees, birds and nature, and the 'better-than-thou' attitude of the royals and their soldiers. The set can be very simple – just some suggestion of green hills and one (cardboard) tree. Your scope for costumes is great: kings, soldiers, farmers, and a cow. Choreograph the battle well, as you don't want any unexpected casualties!

The Set
- ✓ *green hills*
- ✓ *one (cardboard) tree*

Costumes and Props Box
- ✓ *Kings' crowns and robes*
- ✓ *soldier's uniforms (armour?)*
- ✓ *farmer's clothes (brown and raggy)*
- ✓ *bows and arrows*

Sound and Lighting
- ✓ *recordings of birds singing, a cow mooing, and horse's hooves stampeding*

Other Considerations
- ✓ *toy plastic arrows work well (they are blunt)*
- ✓ *the moral is that we each can experience the same thing on different levels, ie. 'whatever makes you happy'*

SCANDAL!

Mary, Queen of Scots

In Brief

Kings and Queens from all four corners come and go, but none have had quite as cavalier a reputation as Mary Queen of Scots. Though she had a kind and likeable temperament, she had little political or managerial ability. This flaw in character was to lead to her downfall.

Also known as Mary Start or Mary I of Scotland, she reigned from 14th December 1542 (when she was just six days old) to 24th July 1567 and lived until she was beheaded on 8th February 1587.

Having grown up in France, she returned to Scotland on 19th August 1561. She married her first cousin, Lord Darnley, but their marriage was not happy. Under mysterious circumstances, Darnley's house was destroyed in an explosion and his dead body was found murdered in the garden. Most blamed James Hepburn, 4th Earl of Bothwell, to have committed the act on order of Mary. This was flatly refused by Mary, who instead married James Hepburn the following month!

The people of Scotland became less and less happy with the goings on of their Queen, and rose up against her and imprisoned her in Loch Leven Castle. On 24th July 1567 she was forced to abdicate, but escaped imprisonment and fled south to seek sanctuary in England. But Queen Elizabeth I of England, her cousin, was surprised to see her, as Mary had once before claimed the Kingdom of England as her own. Though Elizabeth I was sympathetic to her cousin's plight, she could not risk the challenge to her authority and had Mary put under house arrest. There she stayed, in various locations throughout England, for the next eighteen and a half years.

If Mary's life so far had not been dramatic enough, letters were found by Francis Walsingham allegedly proving that Mary was trying to overthrow Elizabeth I of England. So, a trial took place. Though the verdict was a foregone conclusion, Mary Queen of Scots defended herself admirably and appealed for mercy, stating "I have not procured or encouraged any hurt against Her Majesty, Queen Elizabeth".

Nonetheless, she was found guilty and beheaded on 8th February 1587 with the words for which she has now become most well-known: "In my end is my beginning".

Play: Scandal! Mary, Queen of Scots

Characters

King James V
Mary, Queen of Scots
Queen Elizabeth I
Lord Darnley
James Hepburn
Francis Walsingham
Judge
people
guards
axe-wielder

Setting

A dark castle in Scotland, candles and royal flags adorn the walls.

Script

James V: Woe is me! I want a baby son! But I have a baby daughter! Oh, no! I must die! Ahhhhhh! *(he dies)*

Mary: Haha! Now I am Queen of Scotland.
Darnley: My name is Darnley. My dear Queen, you must marry me!
Mary: Oh, Darnley! I love you but I hate you. You must die! *(there is a thunderclap as Hepburn stabs Darnley with a knife; he dies)*
Darnley: Oh, no! I am dead! Ahhhhhh! *(he dies)*

James: My name is James Hepburn. My dear Queen, you must marry me!

Mary: Oh, James! Did you kill Darnley?

James: *(he looks sheepish)* Of course not, Mary. I love you, Mary.

Mary: I love you, James.

People: We don't like you, Mary Queen of Scots. Go to England!

Mary: I must go to England to see my cousin, Elizabeth. Hopefully she will help.

Elizabeth: Hello, Mary. Why are you here? What do you want?

Mary: Please help me. Everyone in Scotland hates me.

People: We hate you!

Elizabeth: I will not help you. I hate you, too! Go to prison! *(she calls the guards)* Guards! Take her away!

Guards: We will take Mary to prison.

Judge: *(bangs his gavel)* Order! Order! What is this?

Elizabeth: I am Elizabeth. I am Queen. This woman, Mary, wants to kill me!

Mary: No! No! I am a good person. Do not kill me!

Walsingham: But I have these letters. They prove that you want to kill Elizabeth.

Elizabeth: Yes. She wants to kill me.

Mary: Give me mercy! Save me!

(Mary and Elizabeth stage a cat fight)

Judge: Order! Order! *(he points)* You are guilty, Mary Queen of Scots!

Elizabeth: Off with her head!

Axe-wielder: I will cut your head off! *(cuts off head)*

Mary: Oh, no! I am dead! In my end is my beginning! Ahhhhhh! *(she dies)*

(All actors take a bow)

Director's Corner

Royal plays tend to be quite dramatic, and this is no exception. The main things to focus on are costume (crowns, robes etc.) and the trial scene with a cat fight, and which ends in Mary's head being cut off. There is the opportunity here for much dramatic humour! Your set designers could go to town if they like: castle walls, heraldic flags, candles or chandeliers, and the like.

The Set
- ✓ *dark stone castle walls*
- ✓ *fake candles*

Costumes and Props Box
- ✓ *Queen's crown and robe*
- ✓ *letters (papers)*
- ✓ *a (toy) axe*

Sound and Lighting
- ✓ *torches or flashlights to light the fake candles*
- ✓ *judge's wig and gavel (hammer)*

Other Considerations
- ✓ *do not use lighted candles ;-)*
- ✓ *the moral is that a good personality gets you nowhere if you can't back it up with management skills*

BETRAYED

The Murder of Thomas Becket

In Brief

The murder of Thomas Becket remains one of the most important events of Medieval Britain, and shows how two friends can become enemies with catastrophic results.

Becket was born on 21st December 1118 in Cheapside, London. At the age of ten he was sent to Merton Priory School, Sussex, and later a grammar school in London, and finally a university in Paris. After his parents died he worked as a clerk in the household of Theobald of Bec who was then Archbishop of Canterbury.

By then his personality was starting to show: a strongly-built, spirited youth, a lover of field sports, hawking and hunting. He also loved conversation and was frank and straightforward in speech. He had good administrative skills, charm, intelligence and diplomacy.

Theobald recommended him to Henry II for the post of Lord Chancellor (chief minister) and he duly took up the post in January 1155. As Lord Chancellor he enforced the King's sources of revenue and helped set up many matters of state. They became very good friends, having similar personalities and interests: hunting, playing jokes and socialising. It was in many respects a luxurious 'high life'.

Henry II thought that it would be good to have a trusted friend in the position of Archbishop of Canterbury, and tried to persuade Becket to take the post when it became vacant. Knowing of the king's fearsome temper, at first he refused, saying "our friendship will turn to hate".

Finally he relented and accepted the position on 3rd June 1162. Henry's idea was that by having his friend as Archbishop he could easily impose his will on the Church – but he was mistaken.

Becket underwent a change of character as Archbishop, and his allegiance shifted from the royal court to the Church and he started to take a stand against the king. He stopped his luxurious lifestyle, ate bread and drank water, slept on the floor, and wore a horse hair shirt under his fine robes. He spent much of his time with charity, distribution of food to the poor, visiting the infirmary, reading and discussing scriptures and supervising monks at their work.

What this meant in practice was that he was increasingly at odds with Henry II. This was particularly so with the issue of Church Courts, that usually gave easier punishments than Crown (Royal) Courts, for example a thief was sent on a pilgrimage. Henry increasingly felt that England was becoming too lawless and that the Church was not setting a good example by giving lenient punishments. This came to a head with trial of Canon Philip de Brois (1163) who was accused of murdering a soldier. He was tried in a church court and acquitted, and only ordered to pay a fine to the deceased man's family. The crown court then stepped in and attempted to try him; Henry changed the law to extend the crown court's jurisdiction. His 1164 law stated that any person found guilty in a church court could be punished in a crown court too. Becket refused to agree to this.

The rift increased, until eventually Becket fled to France for fear of his life where he remained in exile for six years. A brief reconciliation in 1170 was short-lived as Becket was to suffer at the hands of Henry's bad temper. On one occasion Henry was pushed over the top and famously declared "who will rid me of this troublesome priest?".

Four knights took this seriously as a royal command, and set out to Canterbury to confront Becket. An atmosphere of foreboding hung over Canterbury, and Becket even received a letter warning him of danger. On 29th December 1170 the knights arrived in Canterbury. At first they met with Becket and tried to reason with him, but Becket would not give in. Upon this, the four knights wielded their swords and caught up with him near the stairs to the crypt, just as monks were chanting vespers in the quire.

They struck him three times with their swords, and at the third blow Becket fell to his knees proclaiming "For the name of Jesus and the protection of the Church, I am ready to embrace death". The final blow was fatal, and the knights fled with the words "Let us away, this fellow will arise no more".

Becket's body lay in the middle of the transept, and for a time no one dared approach. A thunderstorm was looming overhead.

The effects of the murder were felt all over Europe, and most laid the blame firmly with his former friend, Henry II.

When Henry heard of the murder he was full of remorse, and shut himself in his rooms and fasted for forty days. The king later performed public penance: he wore a sack-cloth and walked barefoot through the streets of Canterbury whilst monks flogged him with branches. He then spent the night in the Cathedral's crypt.

On 21st February 1173 Becket was canonised and made a saint. The number of pilgrims visiting Canterbury grew rapidly and his tomb became a shrine and was re-located to a more prominent position. The shrine, in Trinity Chapel, was magnificently decorated with gold, silver and jewels; several miracles were said to occur at the tomb, and a visit there was claimed to free people of illness and disease. The shrine survived until 1538 when it was destroyed on the orders of Henry VIII. Today, the site of the shrine is marked with a single lit candle.

Thomas Becket left us a fine legacy. If you go to Canterbury you can see for yourself the magnificent cathedral that was built on the proceeds of gifts and souvenirs sold over the few centuries that followed. The cathedral inspired Geoffrey Chaucer's *The Canterbury Tales* in which pilgrims make their way from Southwark in London to Becket's shrine. We can see the magnificent Miracle Window, a medieval masterpiece showing in colourful stained glass the story of Thomas Becket and the miracles attributed to him.

Canterbury itself has a well-preserved medieval centre, with narrow streets and timber-framed buildings. It is not too difficult to imagine the King dressed in sack-cloth walking the streets in penance, or Chaucer's pilgrims enjoying an ale in one of the city centre inns.

Play: The Murder of Thomas Becket

Characters

Thomas Becket
King
Knights 12 & 3
God

Setting

The King's Palace; inside Canterbury Cathedral

Script

Scene 1: The King's Palace

(royal court music plays gently in the background)
King: Oh, my good friend, Thomas.
Thomas: Oh, my good friend, King.
King: Let us eat.
Thomas: That's a good idea.
King: Let us eat chicken.
Thomas: That's a good idea. *(they eat)*
King: Let us eat beef.
Thomas: That's a good idea. *(they eat)*
King: Let us eat fish.
Thomas: That's a good idea. *(they eat)*
King: Let us eat oranges, bananas and apples!

Thomas: And pineapple?

King: That's a good idea! Oranges! Bananas! Pineapple! Apple! *(they eat)* Oh, my good friend, Thomas!

Thomas; Oh, my good friend, King!

(later…)

King: You are my best friend. I want to give you a new job.

Thomas: A new job? What?

King: You will be Archbishop of Canterbury. We will always be good friends.

Thomas: But good friendship can easily turn to hatred.

King: Do not worry, my friend. We will be friends forever! *(they eat and drink)*

Scene 2: The King's Palace

(the King is drinking a bottle of wine)

King: What is Thomas doing? Is he crazy?

Knight 1: What do you mean?

King: He can't do these things.

Knight 2: Really?

King: He has too much power.

Knight 3: I see. What shall we do?

King: *(drinking wine from the bottle)* Thomas is a problem. Will nobody rid me of this troublesome priest? *(the King leaves with his wine bottle)*

Knight 1: We can kill Thomas Becket.

Knight 2: We can please the King.

Knight 3: We can be rich and famous.

Knights 12 & 3: Let's go! *(they slap hands, musketeer-style)*

Scene 3: Inside Canterbury Cathedral

(Thomas is kneeling to pray; organ music plays in the background)
Thomas: Oh, Lord. You are wonderful. I love you.
God: You are a good man, Thomas Becket. I love you, too.
Thomas: Oh, Lord. The King hates me. We used to be good friends. But now he hates me. What can I do?
God: The answer will come, Thomas Becket.
Thomas: What do you mean?
God: You must await your fate.
(suddenly the three knights enter)
Knights 12 & 3: Traitor! You must die!
(the knights chase Thomas around the cathedral, and finally strike him with their swords)
Thomas: Ahhhhh!!! In the name of God, I am prepared to face death! *(they strike him again)* Ahhhhh!!!!!!
Knight 1: Let us go, this man will arise no more. *(they slap hands, musketeer-style, and exit; the King enters with his bottle of wine)*
King: Oh, Thomas! What have I done? *(he falls to his knees next to Thomas's body; lights fade).*

(All actors take a bow)

Director's Corner

There is a lot of drama in this play that may need more practice than usual, especially the murder scene. There are also a lot of props, though most of them are related to the first (dinner) scene. Your props table can double as the King's dinner table. You can use tomato ketchup in the final performance if you like, but probably not in the rehearsal.

The Set
- ✓ *Medieval-looking backdrop*
- ✓ *table and two chairs*
- ✓ *stained-glass window (to suggest the cathedral)*

Costumes and Props Box
- ✓ *food (chicken, beef, fish, oranges, bananas, apples, pineapple)*
- ✓ *wine bottle and two wine glasses (plastic?)*
- ✓ *crown and red robe (think 'curtains' from a charity shop)*
- ✓ *Bishop's hat and white robe (a hat with a cross, and see above)*
- ✓ *knight's armour (cardboard)*
- ✓ *knight's swords*
- ✓ *God's beard and white robe*
- ✓ *fake blood (tomato ketchup)*

Sound and Lighting
- ✓ *backlight for the stained glass window*
- ✓ *maybe a spotlight for the King's final words?*

Other Considerations
- ✓ *don't use real blood ;-)*
- ✓ *the moral is that even good friends can become enemies*

fire! fire!

hunger

The Great Fire of London (1666)

In Brief

There have been two big fires in London, 'The Fire of London' of 1212 and 'The Great Fire of London' of 1666. The fires had a silver lining: on both occasions the deadly plague was eliminated, and the destruction allowed for extensive and improved remodelling of the city. Here we focus on the fire of 1666, which famously started in the King's bakers in Pudding Lane near the City of London.

In the early hours of Sunday September 2nd, 1666, the King's baker, Thomas Farriner, had not properly extinguished his ovens. Sparks flew, and within minutes the building was on fire. At this time, London was a maze of congested and unplanned streets, mostly six or seven-storey timber-framed tenements. These buildings often overhung the street, almost touching at the top. The scene was set for destruction, as the flames quickly jumped from house to house helped by a bone-dry summer and drought.

Panic overtook the city. People jumped from windows to save themselves, and for many it was a priority to flee. One popular gathering place was Hampstead Heath where folks were not only safe, but got a great bird's-eye view of the fire. They saw the medieval St. Paul's Cathedral burn to the ground, as the lead on its roof melted and poured down into the street like a river. A melted piece of pottery found near Pudding Lane (and now in the Museum of London) put the temperature at an incredible 1,250 °C.

Contemporary witnesses included the diarist, Samuel Pepys. As he described it "I saw the fire as one great arch... it made me weep to see it... ten thousand houses all in one flame, the noise and cracking and thunder of people, the fall of towers, houses, and churches, was like a hideous storm... hot and inflamed".

The four-day inferno raised more than 13,000 houses and 87 churches. The medieval City of London within the Roman city walls was completely gutted, and several important buildings met their fate: the City Gates, St. Paul's Cathedral, and the Royal Exchange, to name but a few. Only one-fifth of London was left standing, leaving 100,000 people homeless, and at a cost of £5-7 million (in 1666 money).

But the Great Fire had a silver lining: it wiped out the extensive and filthy slums and open sewers that had propagated the Great Plague. The River Fleet, for example, was nothing more than an open sewer, but the fire effectively 'boiled and sterilised and cremated' the slums to nothing. They simply burned away. Another positive was the opportunity to re-build large parts of the city in a more organised fashion. The noted architect Sir Christopher Wren oversaw much of the re-building, including the new St. Paul's Cathedral (built 1675-1711) that still stands today.

These days you can visit Wren's St. Paul's (for a fee), or the 202ft. (61 metre) 'Monument', on site in Pudding Lane. It is open daily to the public (for a smaller fee) and affords great views of the city as you peer between the railings. Also of much interest is the Museum of London (free) which has an atmospheric exhibition room dedicated to the story, complete with large-size pictures and sound effects. In 2016, London hosted a series of events to mark the 350th anniversary titled 'London's Burning'. During the week-long event there were (free) exhibitions, performances, displays of art, walks, talks and lectures and, bizarrely, an 'Immersive Fire Garden' on the lawn at the Tate Modern.

Play: The Great Fire of London

Characters

Baker
Baker's Wife
People of London
Mayor of London
Fire

Setting

An old, cobbled Medieval street in London with a baker's shop; it is a hot, sunny day.

Script

Baker: Bread! Bread! Lovely, lovely, lovely bread! Who will buy my bread? *(turns to audience)* Hello. I'm the baker.
Baker's Wife: And I'm the baker's wife.
Baker: *(to audience)* Would you like some bread?
Baker's Wife: It's delicious bread.
Baker: And our oven is hot.
(the baker adds wood to the fire in the oven)
(the baker adds more wood to the fire in the oven)
(the baker adds all the wood to the fire in the oven)
Fire: Roar! Roar!
Baker: Oh, no! The fire is too big! The fire is too hot! Wife, get some water!

Baker's Wife: Water? I don't have any water.
Baker: *(exclaims)* No water?!!!
(people walk by in the street and look into the baker's shop)
Person 1: Look! A fire!
Fire: Roar! Roar!
Person 2: Oh, no! Get some water!
Person 3: But there isn't any water.
Baker: Run, run, run!
Fire: Roar! Roar!
(all actors run to the side of the stage; they watch London burn)
Mayor: My city, my beautiful city. *(he sobs)* London's burning! London's burning! Fetch the engine! Fetch the engine!
People: Fire, fire! Fire, fire! Pour on water, pour on water! *(they all pretend to pour on water)*
Mayor: It's not working. London is on fire. London is going, going… gone.
Baker and Baker's Wife: We are so sorry, Mayor. There was nothing we could do.
Mayor: Don't worry, Baker. Don't worry, Baker's Wife. This is an opportunity. We can re-build the city. New buildings! New streets! New schools! New hospitals! New everything! London will rise again!
All actors: Hooray! *(all clap and cheer)*

(All actors take a bow)

Director's Corner

The play script allows great scope for use of lighting – think "fire" and "smoke". There is also opportunity for additional characters such as The King, the fire brigade, animals helping to put out the fire, and so forth. Maybe your children can try writing the script again with the addition of these characters?

The Set
✓ *medieval timber-framed houses*
✓ *a cobbled street*
✓ *a baker's shop*

Costumes and Props Box
✓ *a large oven (cardboard box?)*
✓ *some wood*
✓ *some bread*
✓ *buckets of (pretend) water*
✓ *aprons for the baker and baker's wife*
✓ *a robe for the Mayor (red curtain or cape)*
✓ *everyday clothes for the 'people'*
✓ *a handkerchief for the Mayor to cry into*

Sound and Lighting
✓ *torches and flashlights*
✓ *a light inside the 'oven'*
✓ *the sound of fire crackling, or sirens*

Other Considerations
✓ *do not use real fire ;-)*
✓ *the moral is that out of tragedy comes opportunity*

technology
science

Famous Inventions

In Brief

Britain is a very inventive place, and some of the world's greatest inventions are British. I had to choose from a long list, but narrowed it down to five, which I introduce here as a 'top five' of things we can't live without.

At number five is the train (steam engine) and the development of railways. The first steam engine was engineered by Thomas Savery in 1689, an idea that was improved upon by James Watt in 1781 who included the notion that a steam engine could be used for the movement of goods and people. The invention led to the Industrial revolution of the 1800s, and in particular was much furthered by George Stephenson in the 1820s. In 1821 he was appointed engineer for the construction of the Stockton and Darlington Railway, and in 1825 it opened as the first public railway with its trademark 'Rocket' steam engine.

At number four is the telephone, invented in 1876 by Alexander Graham Bell with the help of Thomas Watson. Bell was a Scotsman who, during his early years in Edinburgh developed an interest in working with the deaf and hard-of-hearing and how they could better communicate. This interest was fuelled by his mother's failing hearing. After meeting electrical engineer Thomas Watson, they finally made the first phone call on March 10th 1876 as Bell spoke the first words: "Mr. Watson, come here, I want to see you". Only five years after this there were 2.2 million telephones in operation, proving the human desire to communicate.

At number three is the television, that 'flashing box' in the corner of the living room. Though some dispute it, the television was invented by another Scotsman, John Logie Baird, in 1925. He was the first to transmit moving images with the use of a box. At first he used domestic objects such as tea chests and hatboxes to help construct his machines. Soon he adopted the idea of the Nipkow disc which consisted two spinning cardboard discs punched with holes. The first transmitted image was a Maltese cross, and the first person to appear on TV was William Taynton, an office boy!

At number two is the light bulb, a bright idea indeed. Again this is disputed, but most credit Joseph Swan from Gateshead with the 'lightbulb moment' in 1880. His house was the first in the world to be lit by electric lights, and his company, the Swan Electric Light Company, supplied 1,200 electric bulbs to the Savoy Theatre in London. Swan was knighted in 1904.

And finally, at number one is electricity, not exactly invented but discovered by the bright spark, Michael Faraday, in 1831. He discovered the basic principles of electricity generation. At first it was put to use for street lights (replacing unsafe gas lights), and later electricity made its way into homes for lighting and powering domestic appliances. Can you imagine life without electricity?

Inventions are really interesting, whoever invented them. Using the internet or your library, can you think of any other famous inventions from around the world? How about making an 'Inventions from Around the World' poster? Or even better, try inventing something yourself!

Play: A Visit to the Science Museum

Characters

Boy
Girl
Professor
George Stephenson
Alexander Graham Bell
John Logie Baird
Joseph Swan
Michael Faraday

Setting

The Science Museum, Kensington, London.

Script

Boy: Wow! The Science Museum!
Girl: Yes, it's great!
Boy: Where shall we go first?
Girl: I don't know.
Professor: *(suddenly appears)* Hey hey! Hello, children!
Boy & Girl: Hello. Who are you?
Professor: I'm the professor, and I can guide you around the museum.
Boy & Girl: Oh, yes, please!
Professor: OK, let's go!

(they walk to the first table)

Professor: Yes, yes, yes. What have we here? Oh, yes – a steam train.
Boy: What does it do?
Professor: It can take you from home to school.
Girl: You mean, like, a school bus?
Professor: Yes, that's right. But this is an old machine. It was invented by George Stephenson in 1825.
Boy & Girl: How interesting!

(they walk to the next table)

Professor: Yes, yes, yes. What have we here? Oh, yes – a telephone.
Girl: What does it do?
Professor: It is an electric box. It is a thing that you can talk to other people with.
Boy: You mean, like, my mobile?
Professor: Yes, that's right. But this is an old one. It was invented by Alexander Graham Bell in 1876.
Boy & Girl: How interesting!

(they walk to the next table)

Professor: Yes, yes, yes. What have we here? Oh, yes – a television.
Boy: What does it do?
Professor: You can watch things on it, like films or cartoons.
Girl: You mean, like, a flat screen TV?
Professor: Yes, that's right. But this is an old one. It was invented by John Logie Baird in 1925.
Boy & Girl: How interesting!

(they walk to the next table)

Professor: Yes, yes, yes. What have we here? Oh, yes – a light bulb.
Girl: What does it do?
Professor: It makes things bright, so you can see.
Boy: You mean, like, on the front of my bicycle?
Professor: Yes, that's right. It was invented by Joseph Swan in 1880.
What a bright idea!
Boy & Girl: How interesting!

(they walk to the last table)

Professor: Yes, yes, yes. What have we here? Oh, yes – electricity.
Boy: What does it do?
Professor: It gives power to things, like fridges and cookers.
Girl: You mean, like, my MP3 player?
Professor: Yes, that's right. It was invented, ahem, discovered, by
Michael Faraday in 1831. What a bright spark!
Boy & Girl: How interesting!

Boy: Wow! That was great!
Girl: Yes. Thanks, professor!
Professor: Hey hey! You're welcome! *(he disappears)*
Boy: Where did he go?
Girl: I don't know.
Boy & Girl: How interesting!!

(All actors take a bow)

Director's Corner

This play introduces the five inventions in sequence, so it would be good to arrange five tables on the stage in a semi-circle. The actors can then walk from one table to another. You may like to dress a student up as each inventor, standing next to their invention, and give them a speaking part. This requires a lot more costumes, though. Hopefully the play will inspire your students to come up with some inventions of their own!

The Set
- ✓ *backdrop of old steam train, television, etc.*
- ✓ *five tables or desks, suitably decorated*

Costumes and Props Box
- ✓ *professor's wig*
- ✓ *toy steam train*
- ✓ *toy telephone*
- ✓ *television (made from cardboard box)*
- ✓ *light bulb*
- ✓ *cable and plug*

Sound and Lighting
- ✓ *recordings of steam train, lightning, etc.*

Other Considerations
- ✓ *do not use real electricity ;-)*
- ✓ *the theme is: 'the wonder of inventions'*

TEENS
children

Crazy Sports and Contests

In Brief

To say that Britain is a nation of eccentrics is an understatement. It's a crazy place, where difference is celebrated and the unique is praised. Just take a glance at some of the obsessive and bird-brained sports and contests I present below: cheese-rolling, birdman flying, and snail-racing competitions, to name but a few.

So – welcome! Welcome to this selection of scatterbrain and lovable activities that the people of Britain get up to. But a quick word of warning – think twice before you do any of these activities at home!

Who would think that running down a steep grassy hill after a wheel of cheese would be fun? Many people in rural Cooper's Hill, Brockworth, Gloucestershire do. It is very unsafe – the gradient is 1 in 2 – and the hill itself is very bumpy. Competitors think this adds to the fun. These days the wheel of cheese is made from foam due to health and safety reasons, and signs around the hill clearly state that people enter at their own risk. This does not deter the many local and international competitors who bump and fall and struggle down the 200 yard hill to be the first to catch the cheese. 15,000 people visit the annual event each May.

Down in the south coast town of Bognor Regis there is another bizarre festival: the International Bognor Birdman. Participants dress up in fancy costume and attempt to 'fly' off the end of Bognor pier. Whoever 'flies' the furthest wins. The annual event is held in the summer, raising a lot of money for charity. The event's motto is "Where people fly!".

If you are after a more sedate sport then snail racing might be your thing. Residents in Congham, Norfolk certainly think so. Snails are placed at the centre of a circular, moist table and have to 'race' through outer concentric circles to the edge of the table. The first snail to make it to the edge of the table is the winner. Snails are painted to avoid any confusion in the rush to win. The event is held on the third Saturday in July and has now run for over 25 years. As you can imagine, there is plenty of time for idle chatter, tea, and sandwiches as the race progresses. What is the prize? A tankard stuffed with lettuce!

Unusual games and activities are a particular favourite of children. On any school sports day you will be witness to sack-racing, egg-and-spoon races, three-legged races and wheelbarrow races. These fun activities date from a time when money was scarce and people had to make do with the resources they had to hand: sacks, eggs, spoons, string, and themselves, in these four examples.

How to play a sack race: Give each child a cloth sack (from a fruit and vegetable market) and get each child to stand in their sack on the starting line. On the starter's order, the children leap in their sacks as fast as possible to the finishing line. The first to cross the line (without cheating) is the winner.

How to play an egg-and-spoon race: The children line up on the starting line, each with a table spoon with an egg balanced on it. On the order, they race to the finish line. If they drop their egg, they have to go back to the line and start again. You can use raw, hard-boiled or plastic eggs according to your level of humour.

How to play a three-legged race: The children work in pairs, and the ankles and legs of each pair are tied together – the left leg of one to the right leg of the other to make three 'legs'. Again, on the order they race to the finishing line. The pair must coordinate their strides otherwise they will fall over!

How to play a wheelbarrow race: Children work in pairs: one is the 'barrow' and one is the 'porter'. The 'barrow' walks on their hands whilst the 'porter' holds the barrow's legs in the air to make a wheelbarrow shape. The porter then 'walks' the barrow to the finishing line. The first to cross is the winner!

All these activities are attempted at your own risk, and I recommend academic study of them *only*. If you do decide to participate, however, jolly good luck!

Play: Crazy Sports for Children

Characters

Child 1: John
Child 2: Mary
Child 3: Peter
Child 4: Sue

Setting

A park or a playground.

Script

John: *(yawns)* I'm bored.
Mary: *(yawns)* Me too. What can we do?
John: I don't know.
Peter: Hello, you two! Why the long face?
John: We're bored.
Mary: And we don't know what to do.
Peter. Oh, never mind. Let's play a game?
John & Mary: Alright. What game shall we play?
Peter: Here comes Sue. Let's ask her.
Sue: Hello, you lot.
John, Mary & Peter: Hi, Sue!
Sue: What's up?
Peter: We want to play a game.
Sue: Really? *(she thinks)* How about a sack race? *(she holds up a sack)*
John: Maybe.

Sue: How about an egg-and-spoon race? *(she holds up an egg and spoon)*
Mary: Maybe.
Sue: How about a three-legged race? *(she lifts her leg)*
Peter: Maybe.
Sue: OK, how about a wheelbarrow race? *(she puts her arms out in front, as if to push a wheelbarrow)*
John: A wheelbarrow race?
Mary: A wheelbarrow race?
Peter: Great! Now you're talking!
Sue: Let's go!

(they walk off stage with happy faces, then return a short time later looking exhausted)

John: Wow! That was fun!
Mary: Yeah! It was great!
Peter: What shall we play next?
Sue: How about 'Hide and Seek'? *(she motions with her hands)*
John: Hide and Seek?
Mary: Hide and Seek?
Peter: Hide and Seek?
Sue: Hide and Seek.
(the children look at each other)
Everybody: HIDE AND SEEK! Yeah! It's fun!

(they run offstage with happy faces, cheering)

(All actors take a bow)

Director's Corner

This is a short conversation between four friends. They talk about the crazy activities but, importantly, do not actually play them (this could be dangerous!). In terms of the set, I suggest a park or playground. I tried to include a lot of easily transferable colloquial phrases such as 'how about...?', 'you lot' or 'never mind'. Using these phrases, can your students write scripts of their own?

The Set
- ✓ *a playpark (with climbing frame, see-saw, etc.)*
- ✓ *play things (football, hoop, etc.)*

Costumes and Props Box
- ✓ a few chairs to represent a park bench
- ✓ *play clothes*
- ✓ *sack, egg and spoon, string*

Sound and Lighting
- ✓ *recording of happy children playing, gently in the background*

Other Considerations
- ✓ *you play these activities at your own risk ;-)*
- ✓ *the theme is finding a happy, common solution to a problem*

RESCUE?

The Titanic

In Brief

Nb. I write this on the 105th anniversary of the sinking of RMS Titanic, April 15th 2017.

RMS Titanic was the biggest ship of its time, famed for its luxurious fittings and wealthy passengers. However, on its maiden voyage from Southampton, England, to New York, USA, it hit an iceberg and sank. This resulted in the loss of over 1,500 lives, and is probably the most famous disaster in history. It reminds us of human fallibility in the face of mother nature.

'Titanic' derives from Greek mythology and means 'gigantic'. She was one of three identical ships running as part of the White Star Line (her sister ships were RMS Britannic and RMS Olympic). She was captained by Captain Smith and, at 882 feet 9 inches (269.1 metres), was the largest ship in the world. She was built in Belfast by shipbuilders Harland and Wolff from 1909 to 1911, and was considered at the time to be an incredible feat of engineering and ambition. She was praised for her safety features, most notably watertight compartments whose doors could be closed electronically from the bridge. This ambition and overconfidence were set to be her downfall.

Titanic comprised eight 'official' decks: A, B, C, D, E, F, G, and Orlop (engine) Decks. 'A' Deck was at the top of the ship, and the decks gradually decreased in rank on the way down with the engine and electrical rooms on the very lower decks and compartments. She was the pinnacle of luxury with her gymnasium, swimming pool, libraries, five star restaurants, and luxurious cabins and suites. She was particularly noted for her Grand Staircase that would not have looked out of place in the grandest stately mansion.

First Class passengers included various millionaires, officials, wealthy industrialists, and celebrities. Let's look at a few of them:

- J. Bruce Ismay – White Star Line's Managing Director;
- John Jacob Astor IV – the richest passenger;
- Isidor Straus – owner of Macy's Department Store;
- Benjamin Guggenheim – famous industrialist.

Second Class passengers were mostly employees of the First Class passengers, plus an assortment of noted academics, journalists and celebrities, and wealthy tourists. The largest class was Third Class (about 700 people), mostly low-paid workers and their families looking for new opportunities in the US.

RMS Titanic departed Southampton for her maiden (first) voyage on 10th April 1912. After brief stops in Cherbourg (France) and Queenstown (Ireland), she set off at full speed across the Atlantic. She intended to dock in New York ten days later, carrying her 2,240 passengers and crew. No-one even dreamed to think that disaster would strike this "unsinkable" ship. Technology had triumphed over nature! Little did they know...

At around 11:40 that evening one of the lookouts spotted an iceberg dead ahead. He immediately rang the warning bell and telephoned the bridge. All engines were reversed and the ship turned sharply. The iceberg grazed the side of the ship, tearing a series of holes along the side of the hull. The gash was well below the ship's waterline. Titanic's fate had been sealed.

At first the passengers were oblivious to their doom, but before long the ship's bow was at an alarming angle. Captain Smith had no choice but to order the lifeboats be loaded. But even then the evacuation was disorganised and haphazard, leading to many of the lifeboats being launched half full. Many prepared themselves to meet their fate. Guggenheim and his valet, for example, dressed in their best formal evening wear and famously declared "We are dressed in our best and are prepared to go down like gentlemen".

Over 1,500 people lost their lives, and the nearest ship, Carpathia, was able to rescue only 705 survivors – just 31.6% of the passengers.

The tale has been told many times and in many formats over the years, and loses none of its fascination, "...for the Titanic seems to have it all, an irresistible combination of human drama and symbolic gravitas" (pbs.org). History.com agrees that "...her story has entered the public consciousness as a powerful cautionary tale" and "...has taken on a deeper, almost mythic, meaning in popular culture... many view the tragedy as a morality play... revealing that we are vulnerable despite our modern presumptions of technological infallibility".

In 1985, after 73 years of silence, a Franco-American team located the wreck about 375 miles (600 km) south-west of Newfoundland. The discovery sparked a renewed interest in the ship, and the timeline below gives a summary of major events.

1985	wreck located by Franco-American team headed by Robert Ballard
1986	exploration of the wreck; 3,000 artefacts lifted
1987	further salvage expedition
1991	IMAX filming expedition
1995	James Cameron's videos for the film 'Titanic' (1997)
1996	attempt to raise part of the hull
2012	Titanic Belfast visitor attraction opened on the site where Titanic was built; various events to mark the centenary

Those interested in the disaster have numerous options to visit, with the most sombre being the three cemeteries in Halifax, Nova Scotia, (*Fairview Lawn*, *Mount Olivet*, and *Baron de Hirsch*) where most of the dead ended up. Also in Halifax is the *Maritime Museum of the Atlantic* which has displays of various artefacts recovered from the sea. There is also a permanent *Titanic* exhibition at the Luxor Las Vegas Hotel, Nevada, which includes a 22-ton slab of the hull. Across the Atlantic in Northern Ireland is the *Titanic Belfast* visitor attraction, housing photos and artefacts. Other memorials and monuments can be found in Southampton, Liverpool, New York, and Washington DC. In 2012 the centenary was marked with plays, radio programmes, parades, exhibitions, and special sea trips to the site.

All in all we have to remember that the Titanic is no myth: *it actually happened*. You can put it in terms of 'what if?', 'could have', 'should have', or 'if this had been done' if you want, but the cold fact remains that on 15th April 1912, RMS Titanic sank in the North Atlantic Ocean with the loss of over 1,500 lives.

Play: The Titanic

Characters

Jack
Rose
Captain
Passengers
The Lookout
The Band

Setting

Inside and outside the "unsinkable" Titanic; outside it is a dark, cold (and icy) night; the air is still.

Script

Scene 1: Boarding the Titanic

Captain: All aboard! All aboard! All aboard the unsinkable Titanic!
(Jack, Rose, and all the passengers board the ship; they look around in amazement)
Jack: Look at this beautiful ship!
Rose: Yes, look! Three restaurants! A swimming pool! A tennis court! A ballroom for dancing – with a glitterball!
Passengers: *(looking around in amazement)* Wow! Unbelievable! Whoahhhh!!! Look at this! Look at that! It's amazing!
Captain: Welcome to the unsinkable Titanic, everyone!
(everyone claps and cheers).

Scene 2: In the Restaurant

Jack: Let's have dinner, Rose. I'm hungry.
Rose: OK Jack. Here's the restaurant.
Jack: Yummy! Let's eat beefsteak and vegetables with gravy!
Rose: Let's drink champagne!
Jack: Let's celebrate! Cheers!
Rose: Cheers! *(they clink champagne glasses, and eat. After a while...)*
Rose: I think I drank too much champagne. I'm drunk. *(she hiccups)*
Jack: Yes, I'm drunk, too. *(he hiccups)* Let's go outside. *(they go outside)*
Rose: Look at the stars!
Jack: They look like your eyes.
Rose: Oh, Jack, I love you.
Jack: Oh, Rose, I love you, too. *(they hug and kiss).*

Scene 3: In the Crow's Nest

Lookout 1: What's that?
Lookout 2: What's what?
Lookout 1: That!
Lookout 2: Oh, no, it's an iceberg!
Lookout 1: We're going to hit it! Sharp turn! Sharp turn! *(he rings the alarm bell; the Titanic hits the iceberg and starts to sink).*

Scene 4: On Deck

(a loud thud)
Jack: What was that?
Rose: Oh, no! We hit an iceberg. We're going to sink!
Passengers: We're sinking! We're sinking! Ahhh!!! Ahhh!!!

Captain: *(he shouts)* Ladies and Gentlemen, boys and girls, man the lifeboats! We are sinking!

(Jack, Rose and the passengers try to get in a lifeboat, but there is no space for Jack and Rose)

Rose: Oh, no! We're going to die!

Jack: Look, Rose, there is one space in this lifeboat. *(Rose squeezes into the space in the lifeboat)* Goodbye, Rose.

Rose: Goodbye, Jack.

Jack: Oh, Rose, I love you.

Rose: Oh, Jack, I love you, too. *(they hug and kiss)*

Captain: That's it. All the lifeboats have gone. Band! Play us a tune!

Band: *toot toot toot toot (the theme to Titanic plays, as the ship slowly sinks)*

Passengers: Ahhh!!! Ahhh!!! *(they swim about desperately)*

Captain: Ahhh!!! Ahhh!!! *(he swims about desperately)*

Jack: Ahhh!!! Oh, Rose! Ahhh!!!

Rose: Oh, Jack!

(the band suddenly stops playing; all is silent, with only the stars shining brightly, for a while, then the stars themselves fade…)

(All actors take a bow)

Director's Corner

Use your imagination – portholes, anchors, an iceberg made of polystyrene, and all the rest. You could go to town with the Edwardian costumes or keep it simple. How dramatic you make the sinking and drowning scene is up to you – according to the age and mentality of your students!

The Set
- ✓ *portholes & anchor*
- ✓ *a sign reading 'RMS TITANIC'*
- ✓ *bright stars*

Costumes and Props Box
- ✓ *Edwardian-style costumes*
- ✓ *large piece of polystyrene (to represent the iceberg)*
- ✓ *an inflatable boat*
- ✓ *an alarm bell (hand-bell)*
- ✓ *torches or flashlights as spotlights on the stars (or a glitterball if you have one)*
- ✓ *musical instruments (trumpet, violin etc.)*

Sound and Lighting
- ✓ *a crashing sound*
- ✓ *an alarm bell and/or telephone*
- ✓ *the band / Celine Dione 'My Heart Will Go On'*

Other Considerations
- ✓ *do not use real ice ;-)*
- ✓ *the moral is the fallacy of believing the superiority of human technology over mother nature*

References

Introduction
http://dictionary.cambridge.org/dictionary/english/
https://en.oxforddictionaries.com/
https://www.merrian-webster.com/
http://www.urbandictionary.com/define.php?term=skit
http://www.yourdictionary.com

Famous Animals from Britain
https://en.wikipedia,org/wiki/Shergar
http://www.iwm.org.uk/history/9-famous-animals-from-the-first-and-second-world-wars
http://listverse.com/2012/08/08/top-20-world-famous-animals/
http://www.nhm.ac.uk/about-us/national-impact/diplodocus-on-tour.html
http://www.telegraph.co.uk/news/uknews/1576718/The-truth-about-Shergar-racehorse-kidnapping.html
https://www.zsl.org/famous-animals

Dick Whittington and his Cat
http://www.bbc.co.uk/gloucestershire/content/articles/2005/06/16/about_dick_whittington_features_shtml
http://www.its-behind-you.com/storydickwhittington.html
http://www.purr-n-fur.org.uk/fabled/whittington.html
http://www.worldstories.org.uk/stories/story/67-dick-whittington-and-his-cat

A Tale of Two Dragons
http://www.bbc.co.uk/religion/religions/christianity/saints/george_1.shtml
http://www.historic-uk.com/HistoryUK/HistoryofWales/The-Red-Dragon-of-Wales/
http://www.historytoday.com/marc-morris/slaying-myths-st-george-and-dragon
https://learnenglishkids.britishcouncil.org/en/short-stories/george-and-the-dragon
http://www.resources.woodlands-junior.kent.sch.uk/customs/stgeorgepic.html
http://www.walesonline.co.uk>Lifestyle>Nostalgia>Welshhistory

Looking for Nessie
http://www.dailymail.co.uk/news/article-4418004/Loch-Ness-Monster-declared-missing.html
http://dictionary.cambridge.org/dictionary/english/monster
http://www.livescience.com/26341-loch-ness-monster.html
http://metro.co.uk/2017/05/11/loch-ness-monster-may-not-be-dead-after-all-as-new-footage-emerges-6630313
http://www.nessie.co.uk

The Beatles
http://www.beatlesstory.com
http://www.telegraph.co.uk/culture/music/the-beatles/.../The-Beatles-the-birth-of-the-band.html
http://www.thebeatles.com
http://ultimateclassicrock.com/tags/the-beatles/

Winning the Eurovision Song Contest
https://en.wikipedia.org/wiki/Eurovision_Song_Contest_2017
https://eurovision.tv/participants
https://www.thesun.co.uk/.../eurovision-song-contest-2017-date-uk-lucie-jones-ukraine/

A Visit to Madame Tussauds
https://www.daysoutguide.co.uk/madame-tussauds
https://www.madametussauds.com/london/en/
https://www.tripadvisor.co.uk>...>England>London>ThingstodoinLondon

Sherlock Holmes

https://en-wikipedia.org/wiki/Sherlock_Holmes
http://www.gradesaver.com
http://www.sherlockholmes.com
http://www.sherlock-holmes.co.uk/

Henry VIII and his Six Wives

http://www.historicroyalpalaces.com
Nash, R. 1983, Hampton Court: The Palace and the People, Macdonald & Co
Newbery, E. 2006, Power Palace: Tales from Hampton Court, Historical Royal Palaces
Royston, A. 1999 The Six Wives of Henry VIII, Pitkin Publishing
Underwood, P. 1971 The A-Z of British Ghosts, Chancellor Press

King Harold and the Battle of Hastings

https://www.britroyals.com/kings.asp?id=harold2
http://www.english-heritage.org.uk/learn/1066-and-the-norman-conquest/8-facts-about-1066/
http://www.historylearningsite.co.uk/medieval-england/1066-2/
http://primaryfacts.com/3431/king-harold-ii-facts-about-harold-godwinson/

Mary, Queen of Scots

http://www.bbc.co.uk/history/people/mary_queen_of_scots/
http://www.dailymail.co.uk/tvshowbiz/article-4434564/Margot-Robbie-set-star-Queen-Elizabeth.html
https://englishhistory.net/tudor/relative/mary-queen-of-scots/
https://en.wikipedia.org/wiki/Mary_Queen_of_Scots

The Murder of Thomas Becket

http://www.britainexpress.com/History/Henry_II_and_Thomas_a_Becket.htm
http://www.catholic.org/saints/saint.php?saint_id=12
http://www.eyewitnesshistory.com/becket.htm
http://www.historylearningsite.co.uk/medieval-england/thomas-becket/

The Great Fire of London

https://en.wikipedia.org/wiki/Great_Fire_of_London
http://www.fireoflondon.org.uk/
http://www.historic-uk.com/HistoryUK/HistoryofEngland/The-Great-Fire-of-London/
http://www.historyextra.com/article/united-kingdom/10-facts-great-fire-london
http://www.london-fire.gov.uk/great-fire-of-london.asp
http://www.telegraph.co.uk/news/0/the-great-fire-of-london-350th-anniversary-how-did-it-start-and-what-happened/

Famous Inventions

http://interestingengineering.com/35-inventions-that-changed-the-world/
http://www.readersdigest.co.uk/technology/gadgets/7-great-british-inventions-changed-world

Crazy Sports and Contests

http://www.bbc.com/news/uk-england-gloucestershire-36412881
http://www.bbc.co.uk/newsround/36836321
http://www.birdman.org.uk/
http://calendarcustoms.com/articles/world-snail-racing-championship/
http://www.telegraph.co.uk/only-in-britain/great-british-traditions-cheese-rolling/

The Titanic

http://www.bbc.co.uk/history/titanic
https://en.wikipedia.org/wiki/RMS_Titanic
http://www.history.com/topics/titanic
http://www.pbs.org/lostliners/titanic.html
http://www.titanicfacts.net/

About the Author

Born and educated in the United Kingdom, BARRY NICHOLSON holds a Master's degree in Teaching English as a Foreign Language from the University of Reading. During his career abroad he has taught in the Far East, Germany, Turkey and Poland. His first book, 'Practical English Summercamp Activities' was published in June 2015, and this book adds to his increasing literary catalogue. He now lives in Canterbury, England.

From the Same Author

PRACTICAL ENGLISH SUMMERCAMP ACTIVITIES
Starhands Publishing (2015)
ISBN: 9780993243806

If you want to ensure your students are not just parroting the right answers but actually absorbing the lessons you're teaching them, then allow educator BARRY NICHOLSON to reveal his proven educational method:
ACTIVE FUN + LEARNING = SUCCESS
Whether you're teaching English as a foreign language or working with students who have special needs, this book provides you with more than 100 enjoyable ways to engage your students in the classroom. Better yet, each activity leaves room for your own creative adjustments and can be adapted to fit your lessons. Student participation is essential, and with this invaluable resource, you can make learning fun and easy for you and your students!

FUN ACTIVITIES FOR PRIMARY CHILDREN
Starhands Publishing (2016)
ISBN: 9780993243837

Planning a party, summer camp or extra-curricular class? Then you'll need some fun activities to liven things up and allow your children to participate and interact in a creative and informal atmosphere.
This is especially true for primary-aged learners who speak English as their second language (ESL).
The materials in this book are designed to help children learn and apply the English language in an active environment, and with this invaluable resource you can make learning fun and easy for you and your children!

FAMOUS TALES FROM TURKEY:
WITH ACTIVITIES FOR THE PRIMARY CLASSROOM
Starhands Publishing (2015)
ISBN: 9780993243813

Most of us have heard of the Wooden Horse of Troy, Saint Nicholas, or King Midas and his golden touch. But did you know that they all come from what is modern-day Turkey?
Educator BARRY NICHOLSON shares twelve tales from Turkey's long and rich history, designed to enliven your class or project work. There are three suggested activities at the end of each section, that link the stories to practical activities for the classroom.
The activities bring the tales to life and encourage children to engage with the story.

FAMOUS TALES FROM BRITAIN:
WITH ACTIVITIES FOR THE PRIMARY CLASSROOM
Starhands Publishing (2016)
ISBN: 9780993243820

Does the Loch Ness Monster really exist? Who were Henry VIII's six wives? And why is Weston-super-mare so dismal?
Educator BARRY NICHOLSON shares twelve tales from Britain's long and rich history, designed to enliven your class or project work. Importantly, there are three suggested activities at the end of each section, designed to link the stories to practical ides for the classroom.
The activities bring the tales to life and encourage children to engage with the story.

POLAND IN PLAY:
STORIES AND SKITS FOR ESL
Starhands Publishing (2017)
ISBN: 9780993243844

Poland is a fascinating country, perfectly located in the centre of Europe, and in this book you will find sixteen stories from Poland's rich cultural history.

Importantly, each story is accompanied by a play script designed for young learners.

Children and teens will enjoy acting out the skits, and will wake up to the joys of Polish stories through practical drama and literature.

ANIMALS IN PLAY:
STORIES AND SKITS FOR ESL
Starhands Publishing
(upcoming – due for release in October 2017)

Everyone loves animals: children, teens and adults alike.

In this book you will find sixteen animal stories taken from real life, each accompanied by a play script designed for young learners.

Children and teens will enjoy acting out the skits, and will grow to love animals more than ever through practical drama and literature.